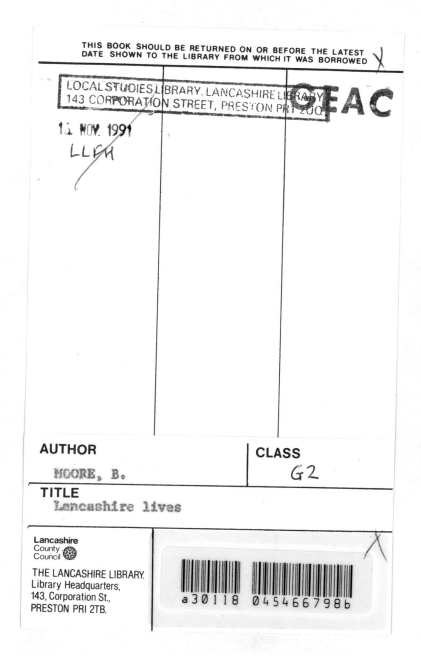

'Lancashire Lives'

Interviews with and tales of some interesting folk from Hyndburn and the Ribble Valley

including people from Accrington, Oswaldtwistle, Church, Rishton, Great Harwood and the Ribble Valley

collected and preserved by Benita Moore A.L.A.

with a foreword by Brian Ashton A.L.A., Hyndburn District Librarian

Lancashire Lives
collected and preserved by Benita Moore A.L.A.

Published by Carnegie Publishing Ltd., 18 Maynard Street, Preston PR2 2AL.
First published, October 1990
Copyright ©, interviewees and Benita Moore, 1990

Designed and typeset in Caslon Medium by Carnegie Publishing Ltd.,
Printed and bound by T. Snape & Co. Ltd., Boltons Court, Preston, Lancashire

ISBN 0 948789 63 8

Contents

Fairbrother's Biscuit Stall

Foreword

by Brian Ashton, Hyndburn District Librarian

ORAL history, the recording and preservation of the enormous store of knowledge of our older generation, is now well established. People's recollections have produced sound recordings in the study of speech, dialect, folk songs, details of local crafts, trades and industries, traditions and other areas of local life. All of these have value in the study of local history and the ways in which our forebears lived and worked.

Benita Moore has already done much work in interviewing the older residents of towns in East Lancashire, and edited transcripts have been published as two of her published works. This present volume is the first of her series entitled *Lancashire Lives* and consists of transcripts of interviews with older inhabitants of the townships which make up the district of Hyndburn. These conversations are fascinating details of the ways in which people lived their lives in the early part of the twentieth century. They also reveal how many 'characters' there were— men and women of strong individual personality, even idiosyncracy.

Benita is to be congratulated in recording and reproducing these recollections of an earlier age.

Brian Ashton A.L.A.

||||||||||||||||||||||||||||||||||||||||||||||||||||||||||

Acknowledgements

I would like to thank the many people who have helped me during the writing of this book and the people who have allowed us to reproduce material already published elsewhere. In particular, my thanks go to the *Accrington Observer*, Eric Leaver and the *Lancashire Evening Telegraph*, the *Hyndburn Citizen, Rossendale Free Press, Lancashire Magazine,* Mr Brian Ashton and his staff at Hyndburn Libraries, Jennifer Shilliday, James Parsons, printers of Rishton, Mrs M. Barlow, and *Red Rose Magazine.*

||||||||||||||||||||||||||||||||||||||||||||||||||||||||||||

Introduction

THOSE of you who have read my first book, *Gobbin Tales*, will know of my passion for seeking out and recording the lives of Lancashire people.

Lancashire Lives—Book One is the first book in a series of three and covers an area of Lancashire from Clitheroe to Accrington. I have tried to find people with different trades or skills which are indigenous to Lancashire (e.g. clogmaking), or which may by now have almost been extinguished by modern technology.

I have also tried to portray some lives of the ordinary people, as many of them have a lot to say which is of great value in local history. Please remember that the interviews are all taken from a tape recording by the person concerned, and that *they* are responsible for what they have said. I cannot accept any responsibility for any queries or controversies that may arise from the interviews!

I should like to pay tribute to Mrs Phyllis Taylor, who has again given freely of her time to help transcribe the tapes; and also to Edna Baron who has helped me in many ways. Without the help of these two ladies, this book would not have been possible. I very much appreciate all their hard work.

May I thank all the people who have helped in the production of this book and, of course, the 'interviewees' themselves for their interest and kindness in allowing me to speak to them.

I hope you enjoy this book and that it will be interesting enough to make you want to read the next two volumes.

Benita Moore, 1990

James Street Working Men's Club in Oswaldtwistle, which used to be known as the 'Tin Hut'.

Three Lancashire Tales

A school headmaster retired after teaching down in the south of England, and he hosted a party at which he told some of his reminiscences—one of them was:

For some years he'd taught in a Lancashire school and one day he gave some children a list of words to choose from and told them to make a sentence using any one of these words. One of the words was 'comfort', and he was amused to find a little boy had written: 'I've comfort rent.' (I've com fer t'rent).

A little boy's pet budgie had died, so he dug a grave for him and wrapped him in a cloth. As his uncle was a vicar, he knew what to say, so he lowered the bird into the grave and said: 'In the name of the Father and of the Son and into the hole he goes!'

A Tale of Thrift— told by Mrs Margaret Knight

When I was a little girl, I used to go to my grandmother's farm a lot. I used to watch her spooning loose tea into the big brown teapot and one day she said to me: 'Now Margaret, each time you've put the tea into the teapot, always take a pinch out again.'

'Why?' I asked her.

'Because if you put the pinch of tea in a clean jar, then in six months time you'll have a free quarter of tea,' she replied.

How's that for thrift?

'THE day I left school I walked to Broughton (I was born in Preston).

I had all my possessions under my arms as I went to start work on a farm; I was fourteen when I left and I have made my own way in life since then. I'd always wanted to work with horses; horses have been my life. My father died when I was eight years old, leaving my mother with seven children, the youngest being three months old. My father had a woollen mill in Huddersfield at one time. When he came to Broughton he started a milk round which covered a wide area. We used to go to Preston with a truck to meet a bus there. We met a farmer who put a ten gallon kit of milk on the truck; we took it home and then went out delivering it. I was eight years old at the time.

We worked until it was too dark to see what we were doing. I used to ride on a bike to Preston with three or four gallons of milk in a kit tied on the handlebars and deliver the milk before I had any breakfast. I went from one farm to another; I was teasman, a horse breaker and stallion traveller (i.e.

Jack Shaw
of Waddington, and his wife Elsie

taking stallions to serve the mares).

Then I was in the army, returning to the farm after the war. I wanted to get married and needed more money, so I started a fish and fruit round with a horse and cart. Food was rationed, so I had to buy a business so as to obtain a licence and an allocation of fish and fruit. The first day I couldn't have changed a pound note. I used to stay out until I sold up. I had three famous horses eventually, and one had seven foals.

We lived in Ashton, Preston, when I started with horses. During the last winter before we finished working, it snowed on the Sunday; it was five feet deep behind the doors. That snow froze and it stuck for six weeks but we never missed a day with that horse—she'd go anywhere! I just let her pick her own way and she never slipped, she was a wonderful horse.'

Jack's wife Elsie speaks:

'I was born in Higher Walton and christened at the same church as Kathleen Ferrier; All Saints. Kathleen Ferrier's father was school master there. Higher Walton was a small village with a good community spirit.

When I left school I worked for a short time at a rubber works at Leyland. I then went in the mill until the war started. After a spell working on aircraft, I got married. I had two children pretty quick and by the time they were ready for school we'd got the milk round.

The first horse we got for the milk round was called Elsie, so we had to give it another name to avoid any confusion with me. We had a succession of horses before we got dear old Brenda. We had her for a long time. We had milk floats until bottled milk was introduced and then we got a flat cart which was better to carry bottles. The old cart was sold recently and I was sad to see it

going down the lane; it was part of my life! People in general were very good. Jack got up at 4.30am and he used to bring me a cup of tea at five. Then I got up and made the breakfast while Jack was 'mucking out' and getting the horse ready. The horses knew where to stop on their rounds; they seemed to know what day it was. One lady never gave them anything except on a Saturday. When we got into that street on a Saturday that horse would *not* wait. It stopped at this house on a Saturday and every other day it walked past!

The winters were hard but we got used to it. We didn't mind the cold as much as the rain. We got soaked waiting to collect our money and we also went out on Friday nights to get our money. We used to have to stand in the rain while the customer rummaged for her purse. We later used the car and trailer if we wanted to go some-where when we'd finished the round. It wasn't as good as the horse, though.

Jack always trimmed-up the horses on Mayday—it was tradition—tails plaited and manes with ribbons. Then Mayday became involved with politics, so he stopped doing it. One morning we had to call out an ambulance to a girl who had taken an overdose (we were the first to find her). We also had to help old people in various ways and we sometimes found them on the floor—dead!

We had a spate of people stealing milk, that happened a lot. We had a good egg trade and sold yoghurt and cream. We had a small, compact round and I enjoyed it a lot.'

Jack takes up the conversation again:

'WHEN roads were bad we used to put 'frost nails' in the horse's shoes. You could hear the nails crunching in the ice. I bought a horse when I started hawking and

it transpired that this horse had broken up two milk floats. However, it settled down eventually. I used to buy horses that no-one else wanted; kickers, runaways and all sorts, but they knew who was master! 'Brenda' was determined to go her own way but with patience and firmness she became the best horse I've ever had—and I've had a lot! I used to buy horses, break them in to the cart, then sell them. We had a stallion, so we got foals every year. At one time I used to walk the stallion to various farms to serve the mares. I once slept in twenty-two different beds in eight weeks. I was a stallion man at different farms all over the country. If a man got hurt I had to take over the horse, some I'd never seen before—that was in Lincoln, Nottingham, Yorkshire etc. I've also done ploughing. 'Brenda' and 'Jubilee' (another horse) were very popular with the customers; they would push their heads in the door as though they were going into the house. We once had a stallion and he was really wicked, a 'widow-maker', but he always stopped for a tit-bit at the same house. That horse hated people, but he was a 'flyer'. We have a trap here still and we go out in it sometimes. A friend of mine who was dying of cancer asked me to take his body to the cemetery on the lorry, which I did. I have also 'done' a couple of weddings. The mares worked up until a week or two before they were due to foal, we let them have their own time.

I've been to Appleby a lot. I bought a piebald horse there. It was about eight o'clock at night as we were coming home. I was offered this five-year-old piebald mare. I bought it, but my friends said I would never get it home as the last train had gone. I got a lad to walk it about and a gypsy came and asked me the price of the horse. I sold it and made my expenses for the day. I used to go

to Wales to buy pedigree horses. One woman swore that her milk kept better when it was delivered by a horse!

One horse ran away with me once. He'd been delivering milk all morning, then I drove him to Woodplumpton to be shod. We got within a short distance of home when he started to gallop. I couldn't stop him. When we got to the traffic lights, he jumped on to the pavement, through the red light, knocked a lad off a bike and went through another set of traffic lights before I could catch him. The straps were broken and the horse was across the shafts. The boy he'd knocked off his bike came and asked if he could help. We got him home—but I made him walk all the way back.

When I first started there were over twenty milkmen in Preston. When I finished I was the last to use horses. We could get round quicker with the horses than with the motor. With a car you had to stop, get out, get the milk to the customer, and get back in. With a horse we could deliver down both sides of the street, while the horse came along with us.

I've sold horses all over the country, and worked all over the country. We sold from kits at first then changed to bottles before it was made compulsory. I've got arthritis in my hands and I couldn't hold the bottles—that's why I retired. Customers used to say: 'Look at that poor horse, it's wet through': they never looked at me with the rain pouring down my neck! I still have a few animals to keep me sane. I must have an interest always.'

Jack and Elsie are now enjoying their well-earned retirement in the Ribble Valley. I hope they enjoy many more years there.

||||||||||||||||||||||||||||||||||||||||||||||||||||||||||||||||||||

Barbara Cullen

Curator of the Clitheroe Civic Theatre

||||||||||||||||||||||||||||||||||||||||||||||||||||||||||||||||||||||||||||||||||||||||

ASK anyone in Clitheroe about the Civic Theatre and the name Cullen is always mentioned; for the Cullen family—father Ignatious, together with daughters Barbara and Marie—have given outstanding loyal service to this well known Clitheroe attraction for many years. Father Ignatious and daughter

Marie are both dead now, so it is left to Barbara to carry on this splendid family tradition of managing and looking after what must certainly be one of the nicest civic theatres in the North West. I went to see Miss Cullen on a sunny day and was delighted with the gleaming brasses, sparkling windows and paintwork of this 400-seat centre of entertainment. It was obvious that a lot of hard work and loving care had gone into making the theatre such an attractive place. I asked Barbara Cullen about her life and work.

'I was born and bred in Brennand Street, Clitheroe, and I've lived there all my life. I went to school at St. Michaels' and St. Johns', then, at eleven, I went to Nôtre Dame Convent at Blackburn and from there to Blackburn Technical College where I was training to be a Chartered Accountant. However, this was in 1946 when my father was running this place and he was rather ill at the time. The girl who was the cashier then left, and dad was rather worried about who would take her place, so I said: "Right, I'll pack-in at college and come here," which I did and I've been here ever since. At that time, my sister Marie, who was older than me, was working at Rolls Royce, but she worked here in the evenings. In July 1946 my father died, so Marie came here to work with me and we ran the place together.'

Well that's a long time—quite an era really, almost fifty years.

'Yes, my sister retired about two or three years ago and a year before that she had her fiftieth year working for the theatre.'

What about the history of the theatre, what do you know about it?

'Well, the building itself was built in 1874 and it was a public hall then. In 1920 my father came in here and opened it up as a small company cinema. He also had two other cinemas in the town previously. One is now Dawsons, the ironmongers, and the other—well it was only an upstairs room really. I don't even know if it

was used properly. There was also a Palladium and a Co-operative cinema in King Lane; it was known as 'The King Lane Hall' then. Both Marie and I fell in love with this cinema so I suppose it's in our blood really.'

Tell me a bit about your father.

'Well, he played for the silent movies. There's a piano in the hall that he used for that. He played here in the 1920s until the sound movies came in. As a matter of fact, this last weekend, the council have just put the new Dolby Stereophonic sound in. So my father managed the small company and he often did a lot of the projection work. Then his brother, Walter, came to work here as the projectionist. With the advent of talkies, daddy stopped playing for films but he had a feeling for it— he could improvise to any picture. On one occasion he couldn't play and someone else played instead. This particular film was a war film showing the Battle of the Somme and daddy said: 'Play something appropriate.' So he played 'Fall in and Follow Me!', which was hardly appropriate!!'

Had they to improvise, then?

'Yes, they just looked at the screen and played. Actually, daddy was a brilliant musician, yet he couldn't read a note of music. He played by ear and composed quite a lot of music himself. Really he was born before his time. Well, there aren't many people who can sit down with no music and play 'The Hungarian Rhapsody' without striking a wrong note—and he could! He was brilliant, a wonderful pianist. When I was at school, I used to come down here with daddy when he played the piano—I always asked him to. When he played the piano he was lost to the world. I can't play a note. I've a great appreciation for

music but that's all.'

Are you more artistic then?

"Well, yes. I like drama and writing. I'm writing a book about my life here at the moment *when* I can get on with it! I started at Blackburn Convent in 1939. Clitheroe became a barracks town during the war and Calderstones was a military hospital. In the cinema it was all uniforms then.'

Have you ever regretted not taking up accountancy?

'No, no—not at all; because the cinema is a way of life—I couldn't imagine doing anything else now. Marie used to come here and help dad in the evenings when she was old enough and later, I came too, so we were both here. We always had what we called a 'Postage Stamp' screen, but even that was a lot bigger than in many modern cinemas now. We now have a two-ratio screen for cinemascope etc. It's the only cinema left in Clitheroe now and it's usually well-supported.'

What about this Art and Drama Festival?

'Well, in 1963 the old Clitheroe Borough Council took over the running of the cinema and they did some alterations—made new dressing-rooms and a new stage. Councillor John Hall thought it would be a good idea to have a drama festival, so it went from there. 1990 sees our Silver Jubilee Festival. We get teams from all over the area coming to enter the Festival.'

What did the audiences of the 1940s like?

'Well, all sorts really. Mind you, there were a lot more films to choose from then. They were by the hundreds—not like now. And

there were a lot more film companies too! Mind you this was all pre-television! Clitheroe had a lot of troops still here for a while, then our own boys started coming back, so we were improving then.'

What about any characters that you had?

'Oh, we'd plenty of characters, but I can't name them of course. We've had a lot of interesting people and those who fell asleep in their seats! It's a far cry from the 1/9d now. We never open on Sunday night though, and we never have. Six days is enough.'

Your family has certainly given a lot of devoted service to the Civic Theatre.

'Yes. We've spent a lot of time here, but I wouldn't have it any other way. The council employed Marie and myself and Derek Pearson, the projectionist, when they took over. Derek's been with us for thirty-five years, so he's given good service as well. We are keen to please and give satisfaction to everyone."

Who decides which films you get and what criteria do you use?

'Yes, it's me. For one thing, I do not book eighteen certificates and, for another, I try to keep it a family hall. I always try to keep a good standard with the films I show, but unfortunately these days there aren't as many 'U' films as there were, or 'fifteen' certificate. Sometimes it's the language or violence that makes them unsuitable for young people and I bitterly regret that. I'm told I'm old-fashioned, but I wouldn't be any different.'

What about films like Walt Disney?

'They were always very popular

—but sadly there aren't as many now. It seemed to change when Walt himself died. Also, they are so expensive to make now. Cartoon features are very costly.

One thing, though, it grieves me that people don't think that the children of today are the cinema-goers of tomorrow, so you must train them to come to the cinema early, then they are more likely to keep it up.

We used to have matinées on Saturday afternoons, but that's fizzled-out now because of sport etc. In the '40s and '50s we always had a matinée for children, but now they don't seem to want it.'

Are audiences bigger in winter than summer?

'Not really, just a flash of summer makes people do their gardens, but then they get fed-up and come back to us.

'Swallows and Amazons' was a very popular film. Today children grow up so fast and I think they miss a lot. Looking back on my childhood, I'm *sure* they've missed a lot; a lot of pleasure in simple things.'

What have been the highlights in your life?

'That's a good question. All my life has been here in the cinema. When other youngsters of my age were going out to dances etc., I was here and I don't regret it, I was quite content to be here.'

Was your sister as enthusiastic as you?

'Oh yes, yes; and really it's like history repeating itself because before they were married, mother sold tickets for dad at the Parson Lane place to help him out. She always had a lively interest in everything too, so when I came in the pay-box here, it was her all over again.'

So you've all worked here then—a 'UNIT FOUR' family.

'Yes.—five really, as we had a brother who was killed in an accident. He hadn't the slightest bit of interest in the cinema, though. He did help occasionally but his heart wasn't in it. He worked at I.C.I. and only helped if we were short-staffed.'

Didn't you have a Laurel and Hardy show?

'Yes, the other week. It's the third year we've had that. We show a feature and one or two 'shorts' and Bill Kubin, the curator of the Laurel and Hardy Museum in Ulverston comes down. The fan club call themselves 'Sons of the Desert' and the top man is a 'Sheik'. They come in from a wide area for this. The Ribble Valley Mayor always entertains them as well.'

Have you any interest in photography?

'No, not really. I find all that I want right here! My sister and I have done turns inside as usher-ettes, selling ice-cream etc. I like meeting people and I like to keep things nice so that people can find them as I would like to find them.''

Well, yes, you can see that. It's a very high standard indeed. Anything else you'd like to add?

'Only that I will stay until I have to retire. I've a great interest in it and we've a good staff, we're all very happy here and like to give good service.'

Well it's unusual in that it's a skill passed down from father to daughter in this case.

'Yes. I've always said that once you get in this job it seems to get in your blood—you can't leave it, it's like show-business.'

You'll have to think of something good for your Jubilee next year.

'Well, yes I'll work on that!!'

Barbara Cullen is a very dedicated lady and very enthusiastic about her work. If you've a minute to spare when you're in Clitheroe, pop in and see the beautiful shining brasses and beautifully clean interior of the Civic Theatre—it's a credit to her and her staff.

||||||||||||||||||||||||||||||||||||||||||||||||||

John and Marion Lund

of Abbey Corn Mill, Whalley

||||||||||||||||||||||||||||||||||||||||||||||||||

WELL, I've come down to Whalley to speak to John and Marion Lund, who have looked after the Abbey Corn Mill—for how many years?

'FOR fifty years. It was built in 1837, and it was water-wheel driven. It was for animal feed

and it didn't make any flour or anything like that, and very little has changed as a matter of fact, except that the water wheel broke in 1961 and electric had to be used after that. It's situated just off the King Street main road out of Whalley on the way to Blackburn, before you get to the Calder Bridge. Because the 'head race' is diverted from the weir, up the Calder, it comes down the back of some houses through to the mill, then under the Abbey grounds and comes out at the river lower down. The 'head race' is the amount of water that is at the top of the stream before it gets to the wheel and the 'tail race' is after it's left the water wheel, to the river again.'

So up to the wheel breaking in 1961, it had been going for 130 years then, hadn't it? How did you come to tend it fifty years ago—that must have been in the 1930s?

'Well, my father and my grand-father took the mill in 1927. Up to then it had been run by the co-operative of farmers called 'Whalley and District Farmers', and my father and grandfather bought it in 1927 and I went into it when I left school in 1939.'

Were you Whalley born and bred?

'No, I was born in Clitheroe.'

What was it like when you went into the mill as a boy?

'The only thing I noticed was the fact that all the grain that came in from either Liverpool Docks or out of the growing areas of Yorkshire or Lincolnshire were in two hundred-weight bags and sometimes more. They had to be hoisted to the top of the mill – either trucked or carried – then emptied into bins. Since then the bulk handling has gone. The grain comes in wagons

and is conveyed without any handling at all. It goes up conveyors or elevators instead.'

Would they be using horses in your father's day then?

'I think just about that time they were using a Ford Model-T, but they did have some small wagons in those days. But prior to that some of the buildings we had were obviously stables where horses must have been kept at one time. Probably the grain, at that time, would come by canal; maybe at Clayton-le-Moors and then by road in carts.'

What was your first job when you went into the mill? You would be about fourteen or fifteen wouldn't you?

'I think I started in the office as the office boy; then the war came of course and men left. The wages weren't very big in those days, and men left to go on munitions at Clayton to earn £5 a week. I carried on until 1942 or 1943 and I earned 30/- a week and then I joined the Navy at eighteen. Then after four years, in 1946, I came back again and nothing much had changed. Feed, of course, was rationed in those days; everything was on coupons; animal feed as well! It just went on as it had done for years, without new machinery or anything. Very little has changed in the mill, even today. We served the local farmers; pig, poultry, cattle and beef. We had a full range of feeds we manufactured and sold in a radius of fifteen miles, I should think. We served Gisburn, Slaidburn, Clitheroe, Tosside, Burnley, Nelson etc. and we catered for smaller farmers. We didn't do very much with the big milk producers, who came to the fore probably this last fifteen years, with huge herds. We had a lot of 'cash and carry' customers who came and took it away themselves,

which is what we liked.'

Have you ever ground flour at all?

'No, but we've ground wheat as an ingredient for poultry feed; it's just straight ground wheat. Barley, oats and maize we milled all the time. At the end of the war most of the grain came to Liverpool and it was all loaded into our own two hundredweight bags and brought into the mill that way. Then as it developed more and more in this country, we got more English wheat and barley, until in time it was all English. We used to handle a lot of Canadian wheat and Australian as well, in the early days, and then as techniques changed we finally ended up with all the English. They tried growing grain here but it wasn't a success; it was too wet. It was drier near Ormskirk or Southport, actually.'

What was this about a poster that was found?

'Well, I have it here actually, I'll read it to you: Reconstruction work at a Clitheroe shop uncovered a poster dated November 1843, concerning the sale of Whalley Abbey Corn Mill. It was found in a shop in Castle Street, owned until recently by Mr Hayter, who was in business as an outfitter. The mill was owned in the beginning by Mr John Taylor of Mortonhall. There were quite a few owners from the beginning. Mr Dugdale ran it from the start and he stayed until 1841 and then it was taken over by a Mr Ingham and Mr Tomlinson. Mr Tomlinson left in 1874 and started up in competition on a farm in King Street, across the road from the mill. The corn mill was run by Mr Ingham until 1907 and then it was taken over by Whalley District Farmers Limited, and they carried on until 1926 or 1927.'

So you retired after fifty years

service there, was it still supplying the grain and stuff when you retired?

'Yes, exactly as they'd always done, though the business has grown quite considerably. We've a lot more customers; our output was almost at maximum production for the type of machinery we had. It would be possible that we would have to have more modern machinery to keep up with production but we were limited by the size of the building, you see. I never wanted to extend a lot because it was right against the Abbey and I didn't want to interfere with anything connected with the Abbey.'

You would have thought that it would have been used by the Abbey, being so close though.

'A lot of people—because of the name—think that it was connected with the Abbey years ago, but there's no record that there was anything on that site prior to this mill, though there might possibly have been. There is a painting that we have but it's not here at the moment and it was of the Turners, showing the Abbey from across the river in Billington and it shows a wheel on the side of the Abbey, but nowhere near where the mill is now.'

So, of course, when it was built, it was built on the most appropriate site with the river and the head race, wasn't it?

'Yes, that's right; it's a marvellous form of power is water because there's nothing consumed or taken out of the environment. The water rights were very strong in those days; I don't know what they're like today, because some river boards have come into being. But the same power that ran our mill would run somebody else's two hundred yards down the river if

they wanted.'

So what's going to happen to it now, is it going to close down?

'Well it won't run again as a corn mill, that's obvious. Hopefully developers are going to make some sort of development on the site. Now whether that will include the existing building, I don't know. There are some people saying that the wheel should be preserved because it's so very old.'

I suppose the problem would be where to put it because it must be big?

'Yes it is.'
(Marion, John's wife speaks now about the wheel.)

'It isn't in the open air, it can't be seen from outside. When it was built it was in its own wheelhouse and that in itself is rather interesting because the roof of the wheelhouse is made of brick and it's shaped to fit the wheel. The wheel itself though—it's a big one. It's broad as well, and the wood had rotted and the ironwork corroded, so I don't know what would happen if anyone tried to move it or do anything with it. It's just stood still there for twenty-seven years.'

Was that erected in the '60s?
(John speaks again.)

'No, that was the original wheel, but when it broke we had to go on to electric in 1961. We were told that up to it breaking down it was the last one in Lancashire to be working. It's what they call an 'undershot'. Now there's 'overshot' wheels and 'undershot' wheels. In the latter the water comes onto the wheel about halfway from below. In 'overshot' the water comes from a trough of some sort from above, onto the wheel.'

You'd have to be quite an engineer with all this machinery then?

'Yes, if anything went wrong you couldn't get anything off a shelf, you had to sort it out yourself.'

Marion speaks again:

'The only time the wheel ever stopped while it was working up to 1961 was when the river was in flood. Now you'd think that in a dry spell it would stop then, but the reason why it stopped when the river was in flood was because the water banked up from the outlet and it wouldn't flow out into the river, so it stopped the mill working. Yet in the drought there was no problem.'

John carries on:

'It was well constructed was the weir. The river came right to this point where there was a sluice gate to let the water through, and if you stood there you could look right up the river and it sort of turned and went over the weir; so no matter how dry it was, any water in the river came right to the place where they wanted it to go to drive the wheel. The old engineers were fantastic, there's no doubt about that!'

So, you have no-one who wants to take over, have you?

'One of my sons has worked with me for ten years; that's Robin—he's the eldest and he doesn't want to take over, so he's gone off to Crete at the moment! The other two have got jobs of their own; though they've all worked at sometime or another in the mill: Maybe I wasn't a good boss or something!'

Marion speaks again:

'The trouble is today, if you want

to make a living for yourself, you've got to expand; you've got to change your ways and this old mill has been run in the old-fashioned way for ages. We've been like the 'old corner shop' type of business in our particular business and we've treated our customers like friends because we've known them so well.'

It's marvellous that you've been able to carry on so long. Have you had any customers that are characters, that you remember?

'Well there have been—but I wouldn't know how to describe them really.'

Marion says:

'They were just the typical farmers, you know.'

The farmers worked very hard too, didn't they, and kept out of debt? *To keep a business going fifty years is marvellous. (Marion answers.)*

'Yes, and for thirty of those years we've never had a holiday, except for the statutory holidays, because we were only a small firm, with four people at the most, and John has been the main man and done everything. In a small business you can't delegate jobs like you can in a larger concern.'

I presume you've always worked in the mill, Marion? (John says:)

'Well, since we were married she has; she was a school teacher.'

Marion speaks:

'Well, I came in when John's father died in 1969. I started in the office to help out and I've been there for the past twenty years! I did the office work whilst John went in the mill and did the travelling and everything else.'

I suppose in a way it's the end of an era? (John answers:)

'Yes, if someone in the family had wanted it, the business would have carried on. We were very busy and we haven't closed for any other reason. Someone wanted to buy it and we feel it's the right time for us.'

It was very interesting speaking to John and Marion Lund. What a lot of hard work this family has put into the Abbey Corn Mill at Whalley over the last fifty years! I hope they have a long and happy retirement.

Edna Baron
(née Mayor) of Great Harwood

'I was born in 1924 and I've lived in Great Harwood all my life. I lived in Princess Street at the lower end of the town and the half where I lived and Queen Street have been demolished, and last year [1988] new flats were completed for the elderly called 'Charter Brook'. This name may have been derived from the fact that it was in 1988 when the Charter Fair was held to celebrate 650 years since the granting of a charter to hold a market.

It has changed quite a lot since I was a child. There is now a supermarket at the Lomax Square end, and now Park Road and Balfour Street houses are being demolished at the present time. I was eleven years old when I left Princess Street, but there were quite a few colourful characters who lived in the area that I can remember. I know that I had an uncle who had a chip shop and everyone called him 'Joe Punch', and I don't know why to this day! There was also a man on Station Road who made his own ice-cream; he was called 'Joe Presho', and he took this ice-cream round on a barrow; really good it was too! In winter he would come round with hot peas—black pigeon peas, they were, and as he walked the streets he would cry: 'Peas a lot, Peas a lot, bring yer pot and I'll give you a lot.' He'd fill a pint pot for a penny.

There was another man whom we called 'Joe t'Bellman', who was, of course, the town crier then and

very well known. It was said that on Fridays he'd collect vegetables on a barrow from the market and go round selling them. The children would run after him shouting names and sometimes they would trip him up and all the apples etc. would roll on the floor, then they'd help him to pick them up. Children can be very cruel.

Also on our street, across the road from where I lived, were two old maids. The children thought they were witches, but everyone used to call them the 'mad-maids'. I know we'd get some string and tie their door-knob to the door-knob of next door and then we'd knock on the doors. They would come out and struggle to open the door. I know they once caught me knocking and I was petrified—I thought they'd put a spell on me!

Now mi mother had a large family—eleven all together, and I was the youngest. Unfortunately three girls died, one as a baby and twins at two years old; but that was before I was born. We lived in a four-roomed house with a scullery at the back, with the stone slopstone and the old wash boiler in the corner which was heated by wood, coal and potato peelings. Outside was a big mangle with large wooden rollers. We'd an old tipler toilet outside, which I once nearly disappeared down when I was very young. Mi dad had to make a seat with a smaller hole because it terrified me. The house was overcrowded, but two of the eldest boys went to Canada in 1926 because there wasn't any work. I remember the Depression but only vaguely.

I never got any new clothes; they were always 'hand-me-downs', but mi mother kept us spotlessly clean, even though our clothes were patched and darned and she always had something for us to eat. (I suspect she did without herself at times.) I remember Park View Mill in Queen Street. All the family worked there—mi mother,

father and two brothers. Mi two sisters were married then. I was the youngest and mi brother next to me was still at school. They were all out of work and I must have been about seven years old at the time. One thing stuck in mi mind, though; when free dinners were made available to poor families at school, they would call your name and then we stood in front of the class and then marched down to Eddleston's Bakery on Church Street. It was like Oliver Twist, with the long tables and bowls of soup and chunks of bread. Just enough to assuage the hunger, but the ladies who served the soup used to take jugs of it home with them. The school children who weren't on free school meals were very unkind to the poor—calling them names etc.

Mi mother always had to work hard; all the washing was done by hand. She baked her own bread in the fire-oven and of course we had flag floors which she scrubbed on her hands and knees twice a week.

We'd also a big white-topped table which she scrubbed. I remember that table had polished legs and she always kept woollen stockings on them so we wouldn't mark the legs with our clogs! We'd wooden rocking-chairs by the fire and peg-rugs on the floor by the fire. On Saturday nights, friends would come in and they would play cribbage; they put pegs in the board and they'd play for toffee—sarsaparilla tablets; things like that.

Mi mother would get a sheep's head and make some soup in a big cauldron on the trivet that dropped over the fire. She did all her cooking on that fire and we had a big, black, iron kettle which I could hardly lift. Friday night was bath-night; we had a galvanised bath which was brought in and we all used the same water because it took too long to heat the water for all of us. It would be topped-up with hot water every now and again.

As we started growing up it got more cramped and we moved to

Edna Baron poses for the camera in Victorian dress on the day of Harwood Fair, 21 August 1988.

Nuttall Avenue when I was eleven years old. This was beside the railway line, over 'Butcher Brig'. I don't know how it got that name; there's a pub over the the bridge called 'The Victoria Hotel', but everyone called it The 'Butcher Brig'. There wer only about six houses, and our house had seven rooms, which was luxury, because it had a bathroom, though the toilet was outside. It still had the big fire-range for cooking, though my mother did buy a gas ring.

I can remember ironing with the old box iron. You had to heat the 'slippers', as we called them, in the fire and put them in the box iron which had a shutter at the back. Then we got some flat irons which we heated on the fire and then clipped a plate on the bottom, so we wouldn't dirty the clothes. Then we finally got a gas iron.

I can remember helping mi mother to bake using the fire-oven to make bread etc.

I went to Ash Street School and stayed there until I was fourteen years old. I didn't mind school, but I wasn't a great scholar. I liked English, poetry, painting and needlework. When I left school I went in the slipperworks at Albion Mill in Water Street. It's still there today, but when I worked there it was a very small company. I trained to be a machinist. I still like sewing today, but in the more creative field. I stayed there until I was sixteen and then I went to the Oxo factory which had recently opened. I worked on what they called 'The Belt-End', catching the cubes in trays as they came out of the machines, which were then taken to the packers. This was done by hand in those days, but the machines were quicker than the packers and we kept running out of trays and you'd go to look for empty trays and when we came back there would be Oxo cubes all over the floor. Anyway, one day me and another girl on the next belt decided we'd had enough and we

walked out, with cubes spilling all over the floor. We went to the Bristol Aircraft Company at Clayton-le-Moors (where the GEC is now) and got a job there. But I would have had to go on war-work when I was eighteen anyway so we just left a bit sooner, though it wasn't really fair walking out like that. Also I was courting by then; I met mi boyfriend when I was fifteen, at the skating rink in Great Harwood. It was owned then by Len Mercer and they had a hockey team. Mi boyfriend worked there in the skatebox and he taught me to skate and after about six months he asked me fer a date. He was nearly eighteen then, and he worked for the Oxo during the day; that was why I went there in the first place! Well, of course, when he was nineteen he'd to go in the forces and though mi brothers were in the Army, I don't think the war had really touched me until then. When I was nearly eighteen we got engaged and mi mother wasn't very happy when we asked if we could get married because he was going abroad. But she kept her foot firmly down and we had to wait until 1945 to get married. He was abroad fer three years and he went back to Italy after we got married and I lived at home with mi parents.

When I worked at the Bristol Aircraft Company I was on a grinding machine and I hated it. I used to sing at my machine because they were long hours.

They persuaded me to go in fer a talent contest in the canteen. (There wer always concerts of some sort in the canteen). Anyway I won the heat and I won 2/6d. I won the final and got £2. Then I was asked if I would join the Concert Party, and people called me the 'Bristol Deanna Durbin' or sometimes the 'Bristol Nightingale.' I appeared in pantos, black and white minstrel shows and endless concerts, and I think fer me, this made the war years more bearable

because I have always enjoyed entertaining.

Well, as I said, in 1945 I got married and I went to live in Railway View (Hameldon View now). The railways were running then and the station was there with its gas lamps, and further down were the shunting yards and the coal yards, and the coal merchants would fill their bags with coal from the wagons the trains had brought. When I think about then and now, there was much more going on then, like the excursions at holidays wher we'd sit on the wall and wave to the lucky people who could afford it. The magnificent steam-trains, blowing off steam; the magic has gone today and it's sad now that it's all gone; the railway has all been filled in and landscaped.

I would just like to say something about the cotton mills. At one time, Great Harwood had twenty-six mills which have all disappeared bar for two. And it's interesting what they have become. The 'Record Mill' off Harwood Lane has been pulled down. Then there's 'Premier Mill No 2 and 3' which Brooke Bond Oxo have now. The 'Albion Mill', which was once known as 'Spring Mill'—that is the slipper factory and one corner of it was what we called the 'Chenille Place' which made tablecloths and curtains etc. Then the old 'Britannia Mill' was where the library is now and there was a row of cottages just below, down some steps, and it was always getting flooded. 'St. Lawrence Mill' just off Church Street—which is now 'units'; 'Bank Mill' which was pulled down and the Senior Citizens Centre built on the site in Church Street, and a new Youth Centre built behind it, opened this year [1989]. The 'Albert Mill', which is on St. Huberts Street, but does actually face where I live on Hamledon View. These are now units. There's the 'Palatine Mill' and 'Deveron Mill' which are now an Enterprise Centre. Then there was the old Co-op at the bottom of Clayton Street which was pulled down and Netherton House—an old people's complex has been built on it. Then there's 'Prospect Mill', which is off Town Hall Street and is now a car park. 'Waverledge Mill', just off Blackburn Road, as far as I know, is still weaving. Then there's the 'Victoria Mill', just off Lower Queen Street which belongs to Hansons Trucks and Corn Merchants. Lower down was 'Park View Mill' now Thorn E.M.I. Then, lower still, the 'Wellington Mill' which is the Metropolitan Leather Works and 'Premier No 1' off Rushton Street, behind the Police Station, I believe, was once a skating rink and a billiard hall. Then I think it became The Palace Cinema! When that closed, a firm took over who made caravans, but I don't think it's there now. 'Saw Mill' is in Britannia Street and is still weaving, as far as I know. Then there's 'Smith and Nephew's' at the bottom of Clayton fields which divides Clayton-le-Moors from Great Harwood. Then there was 'Robin Top Mill', which is a garage now, just off Church Street. There's 'Delph Road Mill' up 'Butts' as we called it; there's now an old people's home on that site. Then there was 'York Mill' just off Park Road; that's now a coal merchants, and at the back are the old gasometers. Then there was 'Cambridge St. Mill' which is now used for storage, but at one time furniture was made in part of the buildings. At the entrance gates on the right, there used to be a blacksmiths and I remember he used to shoe all the Co-op horses from the milk floats and coal carts. Then there is 'Higham's Mill' just further down, then the 'Waverledge Mill', which is still working. I didn't manage to get the names of all of the mills, but it gives you an idea of how once Great Harwood was a booming cotton town.

Another bit that might interest

people is that my other sister lived in a one up and down cottage in 'Campy Corner'. This was just off Queen Street, where Thomson's wallpaper shop was up the back entry. There wer just two cottages and how they got that name I don't know, but of course they've disappeared and made way for a bus shelter.

In fact the whole town centre is rapidly changing. The long-established shop-keepers are disappearing. Recently, 'Tunstall's' sold up after 100 years trading; everyone knew Tunstall's and 'Mercers Mens Outfitters' is, I would think, the last of the long-standing shops. I remember old Mr Mercer, then his son, and now his grandson is there; I'm not sure how far back it dates, though. But now a lot of shops have changed hands and we seem to have endless takeaways, estate agents and bookies. Sometimes you wonder whether they are changes for the better.

But, of course, we have the Mercer Hall and the town clock which are to commemorate John Mercer who invented 'Mercerised Silk'. It's said that on top of the town clock is a snuff box, and that's why 'Snuffy 'Arrod' got it's name. It was said that all the weavers used snuff to get rid of the fluff off the looms; whether this is true, I don't know. We have some fine old churches which have quite a history of their own. I went to the Old Church—'St Bartholomews'—where I was married during the war. St. Hubert's Church is beautiful and I believe Trappes-Lomax, the town squire, gave money towards the building of it.

After the war I settled down to married life and I joined Great Harwood Music Society and later, when my husband died, I began helping at Great Harwood Disabled Club and ended up as secretary. I began fund-raising for various charities and fer seven years went round entertaining disabled clubs

and old folks' homes; in fact I'd go anywhere! I sang, recited dialect and had a comic routine. I really enjoyed it until ill health caught up with me, though I still recite mi poems now and again fer people.

We did have a small Concert Party called 'The Tonics' and I'm sure some people will remember us. I've retired as secretary for the Disabled Club and am now a disabled member miself but I've a lot of memories and it would take pages on pages to tell them all.

I remember mi oldest sister telling me about 'Harwood Charter Fair' when she was a girl. She said on the Town Square would be cattle pens and sheep were driven up Princess Street where she lived and she recalls a cow ran up the lobby of the house next door to them and scared her neighbours wits' out. She remembers 'Great Harwood Jazz Band' who would lead the parade down to the showfield where there were sports and games. I remember the Co-op Field Days when I was a child and we got an apple and a bag of sweets and coffee and a bun. They were all very happy memories.

Edna is a marvellous person. Although she's disabled herself with arthritis she's never lost her sense of humour and still writes poems about the funny side of life and what she remembers. Many people in Great Harwood remember her singing and entertaining and always helping to raise money for charity events. At the 1988 Charter Fair, she, along with a group of her friends, were dressed in Victorian costume and played a big part in the celebrations. Her dialect poems are a treat to hear and I've included one of them in this book. I hope Edna continues to write for many years to come.

Charter Fair 1988

Anuther yer 'as cum un gone,
But '88 wer a yer ta remember.
Wen t'Civic Society, organised Charter Fair
Und Gret 'Arrod sprung ta life like an ember.
650 yers 'ave passed by
Since grantin' ut Charter fer t'Fair
And yer 'Arrod tarned clock back
And fooak from all o'er wer ther.
It staerted wi a procession
Up t'main street to t'teawn square,
Wheear teawn crier oppened t'proceedin's
Wi 'is 'Oyez, oyez' to all ther!
Slaidburn Brass Band led the parade
Wi't mayor und mayoress behind,
Riding in a pony un trap
Togged oop i ther civic robes, mind.
Teawn crier follad them
Teawn 'all bods follad next,
Und onybody, whoo wer onybody wer theear
Civic Society cum next, fain id ed warked aewt
Und as thi passed by, fooak did cheer.
Then teawn's fooak dressed in owd fashend clooathes
Clogs, pinnies and mobcaps und crinolines,
And weyvers and faermers und miners and such
And other fooak dressed oop ta't nines.
Aewr group wer quite patriotic
Queen Victoria an' famly we wer
Wi Edward 'Erson, und faithful John Brown
Wi 'is whisky, grey beard un grey 'air.
We represented 'er dowthers
An I wore a bustle at mi back.
An a little lad dressed as a chimney sweep
Wer carryin' t'Union Jack.
Fooak cheered as wi passed
Took photas galore —
Wi felt quite famous, and
Wi wer sad wen id wer o'er.
Ther wer clog dancers, morris dancers a'n maypole as weall,
Reawndabeawts, swing booats, und stocks,
Polish singers, Irish musicians
And girl pipers playing reawnd t'clock.
An awt way oop main street
Id wer lined wi monny stalls
Sellin' all manner a things,
Liake black puddins, Harwood rock, cakes and sweets
Maybe even curtain rings.
Day kept fine, fooak spent ther brass
Candy floss, toffy apples, ice-cream,
Souveniers bowt, fortunes bin towd
Everthin' went liake a dream.
But that wer only t'beginnin'
A week uv events wer planned,
Ah'll ne'er forget '88's Charter Fair
Id wer summat really grand!

Edna Baron

Mrs Winifred Turner

(née Tunstall) until recently owner of Tunstall's Drapers, Queen Street Gt. Harwood

Where were you born, Winifred?

'WELL, I was born in Blackburn, at Mrs. Turner's Nursing Home and I was one of eleven children, all Tunstalls. For some strange reason I was sent away to a convent boarding school in Wales; and, you'll never believe this, but we had bread and gravy fer breakfast; only bacon on feast day, and a Blue Band biscuit on *very very* big feast days. We were really kept on meagre rations then. I came home when I was fifteen, and we lived on Whalley Range and had four shops then; one in Rishton on the High Street; one in Blackburn on Whalley Range and two in Great Harwood; one on Blackburn Road where the Britannia offices are at the corner of James Street (I think) and one on Queen Street which my father's father, John Robert Tunstall started and Mary Ellen

Tunstall. In those days John Robert had to cycle to the docks fer pieces of cotton and cloth, etc.'

Just explain what these shops were, will you please.

'They were the old-fashioned, traditional draper's shops, the sort where people could get their May Queen and Sunday dresses made, and also their 'brats' and overalls fer the mill etc. You could get ribbons fer hats or lace fer dresses, and I think thi used to employ a lot of sewers in those days and mothers brought their children to be measured fer Sunday dresses er working-day clothes. That was in the very old days, and you got clothes fer the mill as well as Sundays.'

So the businesses were started by your great great grandfather, then?

'Yes. Let me see; we'd one shop in Great Harwood, then mi father's brother bought the one at the bottom of James Street; another brother had the one at Rishton. Then mi father, Joseph Tunstall, had the Blackburn one. They were all the old-fashioned mixed drapers' shops. At first we'd one in Queen Street, then we bought next door, so we'd 53 and 55 Queen Street then.

The first shop originated in 1894 and we'd very old-fashioned posters advertising corsets at 1/11d etc., and all that sort of thing. Ther wer hooks and eyes, ribbons, buttons all good old-fashioned haberdashery, and when I came from the convent, mi father said: 'Oh, you must go and work with Auntie May at the shop.' So I did and I've been there ever since, in Great Harwood.'

Your father was running the Blackburn shop. Was that the one that started it all?

'No, it was the Great Harwood shop which began it all, but the Blackburn shop went on fer over fifty years, it's still there on Whalley Range, although, of course it's something else now. He did sell it actually and we went to live in Rishton; he sold it fer £1,000 then.'

Who ran the Rishton shop, then?

'Well that was another brother, Frank. He ran the shop in the High Street, Rishton. I think it's a funeral undertaker's now, but I've always loved the shop. I loved working there; it wer a big wrench leaving it, but you have to go somewhere and running a small business these days isn't easy. There's a lot of competition even fer a popular shop. You just sort of 'jog-along' if you enjoy it, then realise there's more to life than work, well, eventually!'

Which was the other shop in Great Harwood?

'That was at the bottom of James Street—it's an insurance office now. Uncle Hubert ran that, and he lived there and brought his children up there. We were all Catholics and went to St. Hubert's Church. But Auntie May ran the Queen Street shop; she was a Tunstall—Mary Josephine; but she was unmarried and we called her Auntie May. Many, many people remember her and a lot of the others as well. I've been down Harwood since nine o'clock and people have kept stopping me and wishing me a happy retirement— it's wonderful how kind people have been.'

What are their comments about your retirement?

'Oh they've all been so kind, so kind, they all say we'll miss you. I may or may not retire fully, but

first I want to relax and enjoy miself a little I shall enjoy looking after mi grandchild.'

And will it continue as a drapers?

'I hope so. Not just the same, of course, but they've modernised it and made it a bit more 'boutique-like', which our customers don't really like, but they will adapt to it. Great Harwood is very parochial.'

What did Auntie May teach you about running the shop?

'Well, she taught me how to measure. The shop was always very cluttered and Auntie May was well known fer having *huge* stocks, but she always knew where everything was. The counters wer always cluttered. She lived there, and so did we after we were married. I can remember the old people coming in and asking fer things like elastic-legged knickers etc., thi knew what thi wanted: front laced corsets; back-laced corsets; hook-side corsets etc. We had flannelette nighties (we still sell those, especially fer the old folk). Chill-proof wool vests are now £18 each; yes, the old folk still want these kind of things.

I came in after the war when things were still hard to get. Auntie May kept the shop going though. I remember things like nylons were very hard to get—you only got so many which were put under the counter fer very special customers er yourselves. They wer precious as gold, and I remember a make called 'Taylor Woods'; they were 14/11d and 'Bear Brand' as well. But there was a lot more sewing at home those days; and not so many clothes shops and boutiques etc. People came in fer braid, pins, anything. We had to measure them, and we did alterations as well, all at no charge fer small things er anything really in fact. I never made a charge up to finishing.'

No wonder people supported you then, you gave a marvellous service.

'Yes, we were always open until 9 p.m.; at the Blackburn shop sometimes it was 10 p.m. We used to go and meet mi mother at the bus-stop with her bags, and as soon as she came home she'd start washing—she wer always washing. I don't know how she did it with eleven children—but she did.'

Do you remember any funny incidents at the shop?

'Yes, I remember having to measure very, very fat bodies and you'd a job to get around them. They were usually a bit smelly as well, so you held yer breath whilst you tried to get the tape measure around them. It was funny, really. Thi still believed in ther corsets, though; in fact there's still corsets sold yet—there's still a need fer them.'

What about stock-taking with all that stock?

'Oh my God! Sometimes we had to guess, but it wer terrible really with all that stuff. Mind you, thi weren't as strict then as thi are now with all this VAT and that. Our accountant just used to tell us to pay our tax on assessment and leave it at that. Purchase Tax and clothing coupons wer always a problem. We'd to count the coupons and keep them separate—what a job it was, and you didn't get much for them, either! You'd have to have a lot of patience, believe me. Mi younger sister, Ann, worked in the shop fer twenty years until our retirement; she's made a great contribution to the shop and helped a lot, she'll be missed, too.'

When did Auntie May retire?

'Actually, she didn't retire; she died at only fifty-three, and she's bin dead about twenty years now. She was very straight-laced, though, with her hair in a bun; a great knitter and sewer, a wonderful cook and a great home-maker. In the very old days, great grandma Tunstall had a café and she was a character too; she was Martha Ellen Tunstall. There used to be a character called 'Sarah Anne' who looked after the Tunstall children, and she used to say: 'Great grandma Tunstall will never be dead whilst you'er alive', so I must have been very much like her—it's strange really.'

Your retirement means the end of an era doesn't it?

'Well, yes, but things change, and one lady put in her card that it was the end of an era and that we'd be sadly missed. People have been so kind.'

After the war, did you get more material etc?

'Yes, we got a lot of fents fer making cot sheets, mill aprons etc. There were lots of people wanting these things; in fact people still want them today. We've a lovely little market in Great Harwood; we've never 'stood' the market here, but some of our relations have at Preston and Chorley. Habits have changed a lot over the years, but the old people here like to keep their old ways.'

Do you remember any characters coming into the shop?

'Yes, I remember old Mrs Lyons, a great character, very humorous. When I went into the shop at first I was *very* shy, having been at the convent, but lots of people came in. There was also Mrs Eatough and Mrs Jones; they were characters too! Some people came in every day just fer a chat or to leave a heavy bag fer their husband to pick up. Some people would ring up and say: 'Cancel mi papers will you please er get mi a chicken from the chicken shop.' It was all part of the service, you know.'

Well that's lovely. No wonder you'll be missed.

'I remember old Mr Lyons, the farmer; he came in every day and it was always freezing in the shop in winter. We had a very old gas heater and I used to hog this. Mr Lyons would come in with the milk; he was very old and rather stooped, and Auntie May made him a drink of coffee *every* day. Coffee with milk and Nescafé was 9/11d a bottle—very expensive in those days. She gave him a china cup and saucer, as well, but he never gave her a drop of milk—not a drop.

At Christmas we used to have great family parties as well. There'd be thirty people at the back of the shop. Barons, the confectioners, were relations, and they'd cook two 30lb turkeys fer us and they'd be in a pastry case as there was no tinfoil then. Auntie May was a wonderful cook and on Christmas Eve she never went to bed; she cooked all night. She made her own mincemeat, cakes and *beautiful* home-made lemonade. She even managed to get strawberries—I don't know how, but she did. Everything was beautiful and there were presents on the Christmas tree fer everyone, not just one present but several. I remember all this vividly; we wer a close family. I don't know how we all got in the back room. We were also one of the first to get a black and white television and all had to be quiet when the Queen's Speech came on. Then we all had to recite, and fer this you got yer pick off the Christmas tree—we thought this was great. They wer wonderful Christmases, wonderful, and we did the same on New Year's Day as well: not quite as many presents, but we did get some, though. I'm afraid we've all drifted apart now though.'

Did people want sprays of artificial flowers as well, then?

'Oh yes. We had those fer weddings, funerals, special occasions etc. They would put them on a hat, or a coat or dress. If they wer going out somewhere they'd come in fer some flowers er sometimes fer Easter or Whitsun-tide wreaths etc., very much so.'

You've been in the shop for over forty years, then—a long time, but I'll bet basically you've not changed a lot really, have you?

'No, no we haven't, not really. In fact the people who've taken it have gone a bit 'boutique' and people say: 'You should have kept it the same, we like the old ways.' But progress is progress and the young people have their own ideas these days. But Great Harwood is a wonderful place, the people here are so kind and good-living, it's great living here. I've worked continuously in the shop fer over forty years and only two weeks off when I had the children. I've never had any time off at all really, but I've always enjoyed it. Mi daughter did a lot of alterations fer mi and people used our shop fer this service; you'd be surprised what things we had to do really. But we're in the lazy age now, and it's not good fer little shops. People would rather buy things from a supermarket than knit er sew their own. Ours was always a personal service though even this last week people have been in just to say 'Hello' and see how I was. Another lady rang to tell me she'd found the wedding ring she'd lost because she knew I was concerned for her. You wouldn't believe the number of people who've said it won't be the same without me. They've left ther bags, asked me to pass on messages, oh, and all kinds of things. I'm sorry to leave, but I'm looking forward to caring for my grandson, Michael, and having a lot more freedom. I'll always remember people's kindness though, always.'

An impressive array of cards and flowers from well-wishers and past customers showed just how much Winifred's service had been valued. She will be missed in the shop, but Great Harwood people will sustain happy memories of Tunstall's Drapers for many years to come.

Dolly:
'I was born on Queens Terrace in Rishton but we moved to Sheffield during the war. Later we returned to Rishton where I have lived ever since. I went to St. Charles' School and I left at fourteen and went to be a weaver which I didn't like very much. Then I went to the Rishton Paper Mill, my first job being a sorter of paper on the bench. Next I moved to cutting.

My grandad came from Aberdeen to work in Rishton Paper Mill in 1907 and he was called Robert Macgregor. He worked on the colour coating machines, retiring at sixty-five. They were mostly women in the sorting department then. Later I went to the Bristol Aircraft Company after a fire at Rishton Paper Mill. We were there during the Second World War. After I had my second child in 1943 I went back to Rishton Paper Mill part time but we weren't well paid. The work was clean, but there was a lot of heavy lifting which made it hard. Roger Edge was 'knocker up' for Len, I remember in those days.

Len and Dolly Guilfoyle
(Rishtoners)

We had housework to do, evenings and weekends after work, so I was always kept busy, there wasn't much time for relaxation."

Len
'I was born in Talbot Street,

Rishton in 1912 and my mother died shortly after I was born. When I was old enough to go to school it appears that the lady who was taking me to school took me to the 'Wesleyan' because it was the nearest and at the time it was raining heavily. I had been christened a Catholic but I stayed on at the Wesleyan.

I went to this cotton mill (Daisy Hill) when I left school at fourteen. I had started work down the pit but apparently was under age so had to come out. I got a slap on the backside from the manager and six of the cane from the head-master, which was justified as I had left school two months before the end of term!

I was in the cotton mill until 1935, working on different processes. I met Dolly in 1932 and in the meantime I left the mill and went to Premier Mill in Great Harwood (now Oxo). I went because the pay was better! I was living in lodgings with a dear old Scots woman who provided board and lodgings then. I later went loom sweeping in Great Harwood until that firm went bankrupt. Then I went loom sweeping at Church Bank; Barlow Greenwood. I was called up in the army in 1941 and I left a daughter 18 months old, and when I came back she wer 8 year old!

After the war I started work at the paper mill down the road. I didn't want to go back in the cotton mill because I had chest trouble. I was in the yard unloading straw, hay, anything that would make paper. Mainly the paper produced was for stationery. There were several fires while I was at the paper mill, which meant finding another job until the mill was back in production. I had various jobs but never 'signed on'. I wouldn't, because I think it's degrading.

There was a cloggers' shop, Jack Court's, over the bridge, I can remember. There used to be seven or eight Co-op shops in Rishton. The Co-op building was the finest in Rishton but they pulled it down and built the new library on that site. The Co-op building housed grocers, butchers, greengrocers, confectioners and tailors, as well as the offices. There are still a few pubs and clubs left though.

We had a 'knocker up', Roger Edge, and he lived on Spring Street. He wer paid no more than one penny a 'knock', which meant sevenpence a week! I did part-time gardening when I was seventy-three. I worked for Doctor Barr; his wife made her own soap from bones. She used to boil all her bones to make the soap.

'Dirty Dick' was the rag and bone man, I remember. We saved our jam jars and old woollens and got donkey stones or a few pence in exchange. I've had a good life and some good holidays and I still like Rishton.'

||||||||||||||||||||||||||||||||||||||||||||||||||||||||||||

John Peters

Clogmaker, of Rishton

||||||||||||||||||||||||||||||||||||||||||||||||||||||||||||||||||||||||||||||||||||||||||||||||||||||||||||

UP until the last few decades, clogs and clog dancing have been as synonymous with Lancashire as potato pie and black pudding. Gradually, however, it has faded into the background, until there is now only one remaining clogmaker in business in the whole of the Hyndburn region.

Most of the Hyndburn townships—Church, Oswaldtwistle, Clayton-le-Moors, Rishton, Great Harwood—had one or two clogmakers plying their trade from small cobblers' shops, but since the last war the trade has declined so much that there now remains just one—Mr John Peters of Walmsley Street, Rishton.

Before we 'discover' Mr Peters, I should just like to mention another very well-known clogmaker from Oswaldtwistle—Mr Ted Rushton.

Ted plied his trade from a small cobbler's shop in Union Road, Oswaldtwistle—near the famous but now defunct 'Palladium Cinema'. He was much loved and well respected in the area, but now in his 70s ill health and infirmity have forced him to abandon his trade—which is a great loss to the area, another Lancashire tradition being swept away to make room for modern technology.

Recently, I decided to make an amateur film featuring the 'Ossie Cloggers'—a group of young clog dancers from Oswaldtwistle—who have aroused a new interest in clogs and clog dancing. I thought it would be pertinent to include a local 'clogmaker', so I set about finding one in the area, and was directed to John Peters in his small shoe repairer's shop in Walmsley

Street, Rishton.

His engaging personality and willingness to oblige has won him many friends in the area, and certainly his skill in the art of clog making is spreading. I watched him fashion the irons to fit a pair of 'working clogs' and he spoke to me as he worked.

'Well, this shop's been going for 115 years. I bought it from Mr Talbot in 1954; he'd been in it for 30 years. Before him, Mr Brown had it for 15 years, and Mr Ashworth, who actually started the shop, had it for 30 years—so it's got quite a tradition.

When I started, I only intended to repair shoes—I'd no intention of making clogs—I didn't know how to! Anyway, one day a women came into the shop and asked me to make her a pair of clogs. I said I couldn't but Mr Talbot was in the back of the shop at the time. He heard her, so he said, 'If you want to know how to make clogs, then I'll show you'.

That's how it all started almost 30 years ago. As a boy I'd always been interested in clogs. I saw a clogger once in Taylor Street, Blackburn, and he really inspired me, but I never thought I'd get the chance to learn the craft, as I served an apprenticeship only as a shoe repairer.

'Anyway, Mr Talbot said he's show me—but it was rather difficult, because Mr Talbot was paralysed down his right-hand side. During the First World War, he's been shot in the head, and left for dead at the side of the road, but when they came to collect the bodies—he just managed to raise his left hand—so they knew he was alive.

Amazingly, he recovered, and later was sent to Leeds on a rehabilitation course, where he learned about shoe and clog repairing, in spite of his disability. He couldn't hold the clogs himself—because of his paralysis—

The last clogmaker in Hyndburn, John Peters, at work

but when he had the shop in Rishton, he supervised the cloggers who worked for him, and so he was able to tell me how to make them. He could hold clogs in his left hand and repair shoes with his left hand as well—he was very versatile.

Trade declined after the war, because people thought it was degrading to wear clogs, and also leather was hard to get. During the Depression years everyone wore clogs—they were cheap and comfortable—but as people got more money, they turned to fancier types of shoes, so clogs went out of fashion.

It's a pity, really, because clogs are good for your feet. They're hard-wearing and waterproof, and often children with foot disorders or weak ankles were told to wear clogs for support. Also, children wore them when they were very young, and it helped them to walk quickly. One little girl would only walk on her toes—so they put her in clogs with irons on, and she soon walked properly.

Clogs can have either rubbers or irons on them. I buy the wooden soles and uppers, and make the clogs from these. The clogs I make now are mostly for 'fancy' or work. I make heavy-duty ones for engineers and farmworkers, and some of the ladies at Lion's Brewery in the bottling department wear black-tied ones with a soft top. They find them very comfortable and they keep their feet dry. Clogs aren't all that expensive either when you think they can last up to ten years— about £33 for heavy-duty clogs; ladies' are £20 plus; children's £15. When I started, they were 13/- to 30 shillings. I used to work from 8 a.m. to 6 p.m. every day, and sometimes old men would come in and watch me fashion the irons.

There's also different kinds of 'toes' you can get on clogs. The 'Duck Toe' is pointed and is used mostly in the Blackburn-Colne areas; whilst the 'Common Toe' is round and is used in the Wigan-Chorley area. Men's working clogs are called 'Derbys'—they're very hard-wearing. (He makes pairs of heavy duty 'Derbys' for the Hyndburn gravediggers—with a double set of irons to facilitate digging and pushing the spades into the earth.)

Nowadays, students ask me for 'fancy clogs'—with different colours and soft leathers; they also use brass nails to make them more 'dressy'.

No two pairs of clogs are exactly alike', John says, and you can see the love and pride in his face as he fashions a clog with loving care. Sometimes he makes clogs for the whole family—grandfather and mother, parents and children—and you can tell by the way he works how proud he is of his trade. John is also learning the art of

'crimping', i.e. cutting out and making patterns in the black or brown leather. A friend of his, who is a clogmaker in another area, is showing him this art. He has also started to make clogs in different coloured leathers—dark and bright red, white, green, navy blue and tan, as well as the more common black. There are also clogs made with extra long tongues to cover the laces—these are with the 'fashion clogs', which are becoming more in demand. Rubbers on clogs are used by lorry drivers to stop them catching on the pedals. Irons were used by engineering workers to stop them sliding.

Although John has no sons to follow his in the business, there is one glimmer of hope for the future. His ten-year-old grandson, Ian,

sits by him as he works. I saw him eagerly handling tolls and banging nails in wooden soles. Complete in his leather apron and clogs, Ian already looks like a future clogmaker. His constant chatter was of questions about clogs and what was going on around him.

'He prefers leather and nails to ordinary toys', said John, 'I've always enjoyed clogging because it's not just work—it's also a hobby, and I always think you should enjoy what you're doing, otherwise it's not worth anything, is it? And I hope Ian will enjoy it, too, then he can take over from me and the shop will go on for another 115 years.'

Whinberry time on Kemple End
by Phyllis Taylor

'GRANDMA', look how many I've got.' My deck chair travels were interrupted by the voice of my four-year-old grandaughter, grey eyes twinkling with delight as I was informed that, 'I'm going to bake a pie with these when I go home.' Clutched in the chubby purple fingers was a plastic container which was held for my inspection.

I smiled at the stained hands, almost the same shade of purple as the ridge of veins along the back of my aging hands. As the young harvester raced away to 'pick some more' I realised that I had just been visited by the fourth

generation of whinberry pickers in my family.

I recalled the first generation who made the trek to Kemple End at whinberry time. The outing was as much a part of our holidays as the annual visit to the seaside in the summer, and just as eagerly anticipated.

The family would be up early, dressed in their 'next to Sunday best clothes' but, 'no new shoes', stipulated father: 'we have a long way to walk.' The picnic lunch— home-baked muffins filled with roast beef and salad, with fruit cake for dessert—was carried in turn by the two older children.

I can still 'see' my brother and two younger sisters dancing along the field paths and leafy lanes. Father called us together from time to time to show us the wild flowers and teach us their names— foxglove; ragged robin; stitchwort; vetch and many more. As little legs grew weary the family rested in the shade of an oak or sycamore tree, and the lunch basket was considerably lighter when we moved on again. Stonyhurst College in the distance was a sign that we were nearing our objective, and I felt pity for those boys who saw their parents only at holiday times. I was too young to realise how fortunate those students were in being privileged to study at such a wonderful and historic school. To live and sleep in school seemed to me to be the most terrible punishment possible. The dome on the observatory held a permanent fascination; it seems regrettable that it fell into disuse, in view of the interest in space projects.

Crossing the bridge at Lower Hodder we had to stop to look over, 'saluting the little people', said mother, whose ancestors were a mixture of French and Irish. To this day I cannot cross a bridge over a river without stopping to look over. 'It's unwise,' said mother, 'to hurt the feelings of these mischievous Leprechauns.'

The final climb to Kemple End always slowed down the band of travellers, with the youngest hitching a ride on father's strong young shoulders. Up Birdie Brow, I marvel we ever reached the top on foot—it is so steep—but, of course, there wasn't the same urgency when legs were the chief form of transport. No bus to catch, no getting to Whalley before the build-up of traffic. Indeed as cars became more popular, Birdie Brow was a good testing ground for a car.

To father's cry of 'Excelsior', we reached the top and flung ourselves on the grass for a well-earned rest.

The parents were loathe to move; not so the children, who were quickly lost to sight among the bushes. With what enthusiasm we started to gather the whinberries, and how easily were we distracted, finding great excitement playing hide-and-seek among the whin-berry bushes. If the parents had not searched for berries the harvest would have been poor indeed. But all this happened many years ago and eventually I married and in time introduced my son to the delights of Kemple End. Now his daughter is joining in what has become almost a pilgrimage to this wild and fruitful hill.

The member of the fourth generation of the saga now tumbles an emerald green caterpillar into my lap with instructions to, 'take care of it for me'. Now, a cooling breeze and aching backs remind us that we have as much fruit as we need. We should 'always leave some for the birds', according to mother—after all Birdie Brow is their home!

Memories still linger in my mind as we prepare to depart, but nostalgia does not lessen my appreciation of modern transport; I'm content to let the wheels carry me home. I turn my gaze from the ever-changing view across the valley to the child sleeping in my arms, and my throat tightens with the recollection of that young father who carried a tired little girl on his shoulders so long ago.

Phyllis is now a marvellous 75-plus— a grandma with a sharp mind and a keen sense of humour. I am indebted to her for her help in transcribing the tapes which have made this book possible.

||||||||||||||||||||||||||||||||||||||||||||||||||||||||||||||||

Maggie Smith, Chequers, Clayton-le-Moors

||||||||||||||||||||||||||||||||||||||||||||||||||||||||||||||||

'I wer born at 21 Chequers, Clayton-le-Moors. I went to All Saints School and was in the first Brownie Pack there. I know most of mi neighbours. Cyril Wilkinson wer the first man to bring relay radio to Clayton. Cyril wer always a radio 'ham' [amateur]. He first extended a wire from his own set into the next door's so they could plug into his wireless. This facility was extended all along the row and we all had a small speaker; it wer great! Later we had two more stations and payment was collected weekly for this service.'

'When I left school I had to go to learn weaving; there wer no other choice fer girls! I went to the Royal Mill on Atlas Street. Then we wer all out of work in the cotton slump. Mi husband, Thurston, wer a fire beater, so he wer out of work as well. We only got £1.20 unemployment pay and we had a baby. We learned to value anything and everything we got. We wer determined that the future of our children would be better than ours; and it has been.'

'I have three model engines

which mi husband made. There is the 'Royal Mill' steam engine; and another one—a 'double beam' was the type in 'Th' Old Factory'. (This was on the canalside near where Geoffrey Bracewell is now.) There wer spinning, roving and other cotton manufacturing processes along there. 'Th' Old Factory' had a clock on it, by the way. The other is a beam engine, that was in the Old Corn Mill at Appleby's Flour Mill on the canalside. The mill owner's house was alongside this.

There wer several mills in this area and also a print works. Another mill wer at the top of Victoria Street; the chimney was a very tall one, Carters wer the name. Wellbecks was where the new bridge wer built; Bellshed at the bottom-end wer another one.

This cottage at Chequers is always warm in the winter and cool in the summer. The stone walls are so thick there's good insulation. These cottages have been estimated to be over 200 years old, if not more. The local history society assume that they wer built as workers' cottages originally. The stairs steps are made of stone and in the front room there are signs of a former staircase fer another family. There's Lower Chequers, Middle Chequers, Wellington Street, Stone Row and Hygiene. Mi husband's family always lived around here.'

'Thurston wer always interested in local history. When the cotton slump came he wer out of work and he couldn't get work anywhere. This was 1930/32! Eventually, though, he did get work at the brickworks (Nori). He wer offered a job later in engineering but he refused. He said, 'I was given a job at the brick works when I wer desperate fer work so I'm not leaving now.'

Mi husband had a workshop behind the house where he made his engines. He spent every holiday and weekend in his treasured workshop. I wer always fond of sewing and later got a job as a sewer at £2 a week plus bonus. I worked there (on Owen Street) fer thirty-four years. Thurston wanted to go in the Navy during the war and with his love of engineering he could have made it his career. However, the brickworks wer a 'reserved' occupation. Mi husband had a very inventive mind and came up with all sorts of 'brilliant' ideas so that Nori brickworks could make all kinds of modifications fer use in the war. He made small rings fer 'Dubai' from Nori brick, which is very hard. He also made the dyes. He made a machine which could pick up a quantity of rings at once. Mi grandson, Adam, has done well in engineering; his grandfather would have bin proud of him. The things mi grandson forecasts fer the future are fantastic; the technology today is unbelievable.

Mi husband went to work as a manager of a brickworks in Wales, but he didn't stop—he wanted to get back to his inventor's shed. I had a great mother-in-law and a great mother. We always had a babysitter if we wanted to go out anywhere. Once thi went on a wagonette picnic and stopped at a pub in Clitheroe. There was a family called Burgess who lived on Church Street and ther wer two sisters who never married, but they wer good dressmakers, though. Thi had a brother who was an engineer at the Corn Mill. Mi husband went to see the engine before the mill wer demolished and he decided to make a model of it. He measured the dimensions of the engine, then started on it. He always did a good job on anything he did.

Miss Doyle, who wer headmistress of St. Mary's School, was the daughter of the engineer at the Corn Mill. When Miss Doyle (who was ninety years old) saw the model of the engine Thurston had made she cried! Mi husband had no formal training as an engineer, he just picked it up himself.'

'Any house painting wer my job, or if a handle came off a door, it stopped off. He had no time fer that sort of thing—you know the saying: 'you can always tell a joiner because his back door's hanging off.' Thurston loved pies and cakes, so I threatened to stop all cakes and pie making until the door handle wer put on.

He made a brick-making machine model to scale; it produced miniature bricks with the 'Nori' stamp on! That model went on show to Bury and lots of workers from the brick yard came to see the machine. When mi husband died, I covered the machines with cellophane. In winter it wer damp as we had no heat on; also the machines wer hidden away. Armitage, who now owns Nori, suggested we allow the brick-making machine to be housed at the museum at Wakefield, so we agreed and now it can be plugged in to keep warm and is on show as the oldest model. The new brick works in Wakefield is run by just seven men. So the oldest machine is now in the newest brick yard, funny that isn't it?'

'I've always been a sewer so now I just do alterations. Mi daughter is a marvellous painter; she's painted some beautiful watercolours.'

'I just remembered the old wagonettes; mi grandfather had an album of wagonette pictures. He would show us the pictures but we weren't allowed to touch them. They are now family heirlooms. We used to have canal picnics as well, from Clayton to Rose Grove. At Rose Grove we had a field day, then sailed back to Clayton; it wer great.'

'Thurston made a sun dial and it's now in the garden. 'Meyrick' wer mi maiden name. It's a Welsh name from mi grandfather who wer a stone mason.'

'There wer a cloggers; Harry Briggs, in the wooden hut on Barnes Street at Clayton. The Co-op-cloggers wer back to the hut as well. Ther wer also a laundry in Clayton—'Eagle Works' wer its name and it wer right down Barnes Street. The big house wer rented to Fred Skinner and 'Victoria' was a dance hall in Clayton. It had a genuine maple wood floor and wer known as 'The Vic'. Ther wer also boxing matches promoted at the Vic. Later the Vic changed to a bingo hall and it 'went like a bomb.'

People have been from all over the world to see these model engines. An old bell from All Saints School was unearthed and Thurston restored this bell and returned it to the school in lovely condition.'

Maggie still lives in Chequers, near to where she was born. What a talented family these Smiths are—to be sure. If he'd been alive today, Thurston Smith would be much sought after as a first-class engineer. Maggie herslf is still a lovely sewer and has a very lively mind. She keeps herself busy and it was a privilege to speak to her. She also showed me her husband's old workshop in the garden shed which she's left just as he left everything himself. I hope his grandson can make use of it some day.

||||||||||||||||||||||||||||||||||||||||||||||||||

Clarrie Greenwood

Cheese stall owner on Accrington Market

||||||||||||||||||||||||||||||||||||||||||||||||||||||||||||||||||||||||||||||||||||||||||

'WELL, I wer born up Woodnook in Accrington. I went half-time when I wer twelve years old—in a cotton mill.'

It wer cheap labour, exploitation of the young then. The bosses med ther money from the blood and sweat of ther employees n' them days. The owner started out as a tackler, but he saved and gradually worked his way up to become an employer. I got £1 per week when I first started. After about six years in the mill, I left to become a lorry driver. I went to Manchester wi' a load o' cloth and came back wi' a load o' cotton. Eventually I got out of that 'whirlpool' and went bus driving fer Accrington Corporation.'

You've had a chequered career?

'I have that! Later a got married; she wer a grand lass, our Evelyn. Her aunt wer in the 'cheese business' and she set us up in the same business as herself. We bought the cheese from reputable dealers; it wer all farm cheese then, you know.'

Where did you start the business?

'Well believe it er not, I started in Skipton; just on Saturday's. Then

suddenly, a stall came to let in the Markct Hall in Accrington. I applied fer it and got it, and that wer one of the best moves I made in mi life!'

What kind of cheese did you sell?

'Oh, you didn't get confused i' them days! Ther wer only three sorts: Lancs. mild, Lancs. tasty and Lancs. medium!'

Did you have to go in the army?

'Well I've a 'trick' leg. I wanted to go in the navy and I went fer a medical in Blackburn. The doctor looked at me and he said, "You're lop-sided." He says, "No you'll not do fer the navy." "How about the army, then?" I asked. "No," he said, "Yer not really fit fer army service at all." "Thanks very

much," I said. So I joined the Home Guard and I worked a damned sight harder there than I did as a bus driver! After a shift on the buses, I went to the drill hall fer practice—'throwing bombs' and firing guns. Wi became fairly reasonable soldiers and wi used to have army exercises at weekend camps. Then volunteers wer requested fer bus drivers to go to London as drivers, at the height of the bombing raids. I went down there and it wer "lovely; bang, bang, bang." That just about sums up mi army career which wer pretty stale!'

Tell me about your life in the Market Hall in Accrington.

'Well, it wer hard work. Cheese wer rationed then—about two ounces per week per book. I went on the buses to subsidise the stall,

Clarrie Greenwood outside his cheese stall in Accrington Market Hall

which wer making nothing at that time. After the war, when restrictions eased up, I opened another cheese stall on the outside market and it's still there yet! After I lost mi wife, I lost interest in the business. When you lose yer partner, there isn't much left, is there?

There are a lot o' different sorts o' cheese now; some imported and some produced here, on our own doorstep. Lancashire cheese isn't necessarily made in Lancashire; it could be made in Cheshire. Cheese is made from milk which is basically the same in any county; but it's made to prescription.'

How do you like the more modern stalls now, on Accrington market?

'Oh it's tons better now than the old canvas topped stalls. It (the market, that is) once got on fire

and the whole lot went up in smoke in about two minutes! I suppose it wer a good ending really, because the market was rebuilt in concrete and steel in the early '60s. The early generation of market tenants must have been very hardy, standing outside in all sorts of weather.Trying to sell yer goods—it's murder!'

Did you have any 'characters' amongst your customers?

'Yes. I had two blind people who used to come quite regularly. They knew exactly where the stall was and where to stand waiting fer their turn to be served. One of them used to deliver newspapers; I don't know how he did it! He had a stick and he 'waggled it about' a lot. He seemed to have the ability to 'home in' on whatever he wanted. Thomas Fielding was his name. Anyway you've come to see me on

a great day, luv, it's blowing like hell.'

What about entertainment? Did you go to the Hippodrome? (The local theatre)

'Yes, and there wer some damn good acts on there. I always went to Accrington Amateurs' shows as well. They had some marvellous singers, solo and choral singing used to make the old Hippodrome ring. It cost sixpence in the gallery and two-and-six in the stalls. The Hippodrome wer always clean and well-kept; of course it's gone now. To me there's nothing permanent in this world; people come and go and buildings are demolished. Audrey, mi daughter, looks after the stall now, she also makes meals fer me and does mi washing because I've got a bit lazy. I have grandchildren but they live up in Cumbria at Appleby. I've been to

Accrington Market Hall as it was in 1958

Appleby Fair several times. They chuck th'orses in t' river there. They cover 'em wi washing-up liquid then scrub 'em down; it's a nice day out. I used to do good business in Skipton Market, which is still one of the old traditional street markets. Farmers and agricultural workers wer amongst mi customers and they used to like a pint. By the way, they preferred

really strong cheese! I had two farm suppliers and I've watched the cheese being made on the premises. I know how it was made; with great care and caution. Making cheese involves a lot of 'know how' and the ingredients have to be just right. It's fascinating to watch!'

How was the mild and mature

cheese made?

'It's a question of age; same as me, I'm mature and 'tasty'. You are 'medium'. After the cheese solidified, it wer cut into slices and allowed to drain before being put in the presses wer all the whey (liquid) wer squeezed out of the curd. This 'curds and whey' wer made use of by the cheese producers who also kept pigs; and pigs love the liquids from cheese. Bacon is a 'by product' of cheese - at least it wer in mi younger days.

And on that happy note we'll end—I'm tired.'

What a wonderful character Clarrie still is—I could have talked to him for hours more. His cheese stalls are still a popular venue on the modern Accrington Market, and 'Greenwoods' is a by-word for lovely Lancashire cheeses, as well as many other delicious varieties.

IIIIIIIIIIIIIIIIIIIIIIIIIIIIIIIIIIIIIIIIIIIIIIIIIIIIII

The Southworth family

IIIIIIIIIIIIIIIIIIIIIIIIIIIIIIIIIIIIIIIIIIIIIIIIIIIIIIIIIIIIIIIIIIIIIIIIIIIIIIIIIIIIIIIIIIIIIIIIIIIIIIIIIIIIIIIIIIIIIIIIIIIIIIIIIIIIII

THE name of Southworth has become synonymous with good, nourishing tripe in both Accrington and Haslingden, over the past decades. Tripe has always been a favourite dish with Lancastrians, and Southworths have, for many years, had stalls on both Accrington and Haslingden markets. The business has now changed hands,

but there are three members of the Southworth family still alive, and I was lucky enough to be able to contact them all.

Annie Southworth

Where were you born, Annie?

'Rawtenstall. I went to school at Alder Grange. I was only young when we came to live in Accrington where I went to St. James's School. I went to learn weaving when I was twelve and full-time at fourteen, at a mill in Grange Lane. I left there on doctor's orders. He said that I needed more fresh air. However, I went to another mill in Haslingden where I worked for over thirty years. After a spell in hospital, I didn't go back in the mill. My husband was working at the tripe works in Hyndburn Road, but he left because the pay was low. He was part of the Southworth family, famous for tripe. The winters were bad and traders were often stranded on the 'tops' because their vehicles got stuck in the snow and ice. I helped with the market stalls selling tripe for quite a while, though.'

Annie still helps on one of the tripe stalls at Haslingden Market, two days per week.

Tommy Southworth

'I was born in Oak Street in Accrington and there were six children in my family. I went to St. James's School and I was working when I was going to school. My parents were Robert and Annie Southworth, and it was another Robert, my great-grandfather, who started the tripe business in 1850. The family originated from Wiswell, near Whalley, and came to Accrington where they started the business, which has been handed down from father to son ever since. I worked on the black pudding stall when I was eight years old, this being my father's stall. The first stall our family had was in Abbey Street in Accrington. Later we moved to a spot near the Town Hall. At that time the stall was a green wooden hut on wheels. We had to move the stall on a Sunday down to the tripe works on Croft Street. The original works was behind the Warners Arms Inn, though.'

What was done at the tripe works?

'Well, the tripe was cleaned and

cooked ready for the customers.'

Where did you obtain the tripe?

'From the slaughter houses; tripe is the stomach of a cow. We collected them, then they were scalded and scraped, then cooked and dressed. We got the tripe from a slaughter house in Moreton Street, off Hyndburn Road. When we entered the Common Market, Accrington slaughter house was closed down and eventually we had to go to Carlisle for supplies and even as far as Lockerbie in Scotland.'

Tell us how you made black puddings.

'They are made with groats (oats with the husks removed), blood, fat, herbs, onions and seasoning. They were made by hand and the mixture was fed through a funnel into the skin. The skin is the intestine of a cow. We had a gas boiler behind the stall and we sold hot or cold black puddings. People used to eat them at the stall.

There were fruit stalls on the market, also Seth Sutcliffe, the auctioneer. He stood under the covered market at the bottom of Infant Street. This was when the stalls were exposed to the elements—the only protection was a heavy, canvas sheet over the top.

I left school when I was thirteen, after working half time for a year. I then worked full time in the tripe works in Accrington. I did anything and everything! Before I left school I used to take the pony and cart to Scaitcliffe pit fer a load o' coal, this was taken by wheelbarrow into the works. (This was before I went to school.) All boys had to work; they were as strong at fourteen, as grown men are today. During the First World War, a farmer came to the school. He wanted volunteer boys to go to Green Howarth to dig up potatoes and they were never short of volunteers because the farmers' wife made us a meal

which was very welcome in the days when food was scarce.'

Tell us about the process of dressing tripe.

'Well, after we got the cows' stomachs to the works, they had to be washed, then scalded and scraped. The tripe is cooked, cooled and then bleached and dressed of all the skin and fat. We opened a branch in North Shields which was run by my brother. We also had a stall on the market in Haslingden. I worked there when I was half-time, at twelve years old. When I first started there, I had to take the tripe up in a big dustbin on the tram. The tram driver gave me a lift off at the bottom of Regent Street and I then had to 'dolly' the bin up to the market in Deardengate. The new motorway meant the closure of our business because we were in the way.'

Were you called-up in the second war?

'No, it was a reserved occupation. We had two ponies and carts which I used to deliver tripe to the shops. I finished on the market when I was seventy after suffering two seizures. There's not the same demand now for tripe and black puddings, although they are nourishing foods. Today's food is mostly frozen or canned—anything for convenience. Life was more interesting in the past than it is now. There wer more going on and there wer more characters about. I couldn't leave the stall if I wanted to go to the toilet. I had to 'run like mad' to the bottom of Dutton Street.'

What do you think about this new shopping precinct?

'It's fine, but I think it's unfortunate when you see all the empty shops in Accrington, and more to come—imagine a business like

Catlows closing down, it's very sad. I remember Catlows starting with a stall on the market, near to the fish market. The fish market hasn't altered much; there used to be Bramwells and Fletchers from Fleetwood; there wer Sarsfields as well, who worked for one of the other fishmongers then started up on his own.

We had some cold winters. Sometimes the wind would blow the gas out from under the boiler. On one occasion, as I was re-lighting it—it exploded! My father never closed before midnight on a Saturday. Always, at ten o'clock, he went fer a drink, leaving me on mi own. One chap came to the stall; he was three parts drunk and he said:

'A quarter of dark tripe.'

I said, 'We have no dark tripe.'

'You're a liar,' he said, 'you have.'

I said, 'Here, have a look,' an' it wer the dishcloth.

We were busy after the pubs closed, it was said that a plate of tripe sobered 'em up.'

What is tripe seam?

'The cow's stomach has three parts and seam is the meaty part, the dark tripe is another complete stomach. There were a few pubs near the market—The Commercial, The Thwaites Arms at the Blackburn Road end of what is now Broadway. Tripe wer fourpence a pound, black puddings wer a penny or halfpenny. There used to be a cart which wer taken round the streets from which hot peas wer sold. These peas wer black and wer much sought after. The hand-cart was pulled around by a salesman; he had a bucket-fire wi' a pan on. Every Monday morning, a chap came round selling dried fish which he carried in a basket on his head. On a Wednesday, it was the crumpet man, who also had a basket on his head. I remember the fire at

Baileys when several young women died. Most of the stall-holders were local people. I remember Fureys, Nadins and Schattens, who sold poultry and eggs.'

Tommy is a grand old man now living in retirement.

Elsie Lambert (née Southworth)

Elsie was at the tripe stall for fifty years. I wasn't going to ask her age but she says she's 76. Now where were you born and bred Elsie?

'In Accrington in Oak Street, we lived at the top, but the tripe shop was at the bottom of the street.'

So whose was the tripe shop, then?

'My father's. He was called Robert Southworth; well his father started off the business; my grandfather who was called Robert, too.'

So, it was down at the bottom of Oak Street, then?

'Yes. The shop was in Oak Street and we worked from there at the market.'

Did you prepare the tripe there as well?

'No, that was in Croft Street, the works where the tripe come to.'

So you had a little works in Croft Street as well, and was the shop at Oak Street when you were born?

'Yes it was, for some time before.'

Of course you've an older brother Tommy, so he'd be

down there before you?

'Yes, and when dad died in 1940 he ran it. Dad died during an air raid from shock, and when he died our Tom took over. Of course my dad and our Tom had always worked together anyway. St. James's was the school I attended.'

Did you attend the church as well?

'Oh yes, and I was married there, too—50 years ago.'

Was it expected that you would go into the tripe business because you were a Southworth?

'No. As it happened I worked in the mill. I left school at 14 and went into the mill down Union Street—I can't think of the name. I worked there and then I went on two looms and worked up to three looms and then the factory closed down. They moved me then from Union Street to a new factory in Church Street. I worked there and they closed down about twelve months after!'

So this would be in the 1920s then?

'Yes. Well after that I went to the Labour Exchange and they said they couldn't do anything for me. They said my father was in business so I'd better get my father to employ me. So my dad says: 'right you can come and work on the market.' So that's how I came to work for my dad!'

So that would be 1925 or 26—right?

'Oh yes, the Depression was on, and we had the war you know. We had the queues with the 2 ounces of dripping for every customer. My sister Annie the eldest, she was the main one on the stall, (not my sister-in-law, also called Annie), my

Accrington Market Hall in 1989

real sister Annie and her husband Jim Cooke.'

They were the ones I knew; she wore glasses, didn't she?

'That's right. Those two were very well-known then, our Annie and I and Jim. Then we employed another young woman, a Mrs Taylor, to help us, and us four ran the stall all during the war and everything, and there were queues every day.'

That is the Second World War you're talking about?

'That's right.'

Now, going back a bit to when you had your place to prepare the tripe, did your dad or Tom have to go and get the cow's stomachs or whatever they are?

'Oh yes. They went all over. Penrith we got a lot from and various other places, and our own abattoirs in Moreton Street—we got a lot from there as well. When that closed we had to go out and get it from other places. Our Tom used to go and fetch it.'

Had you only one brother?

'No, I had an older brother called Robert in North Shields with the same business in tripe.'

Why did he leave Accrington?

'My father had a brother in North Shields with a tripe business. He wasn't making a do with it; he was drinking, I think, and the business went to pot, so he just packed his bags and went abroad.'

What, and left it?

'Yes—left it as it stood! Well while it was empty like that, my father got my eldest brother to get married sharpish and go and live up there and run it.'

Marvellous! So you're a right 'Tripey' family.

'Yes, and it's still going, and his son's running it now. He had two sons, one of them was knocked-out of it, but the younger son has it yet and it's thriving up there.'

Are they on North Shields market then?

'Oh no, they supply the shops, they don't do anything else, only that up there.'

How marvellous, a bit of Accrington's gone up there then?

'Yes, it's been up there for years and doing well.'

So going back, when you went on the market at 16, your father and your brother were running the shop in Oak Street?

'Our Tom was, yes—he was very good.'

And you were put on the market stall you used to have the green stalls with wheels on, didn't you?

'Yes, and the little wooden hut at the corner of the Town Hall, that's where we started. We were well-known.'

And Annie, your elder sister, who presumably was married to Jim by then, was there as well, wasn't she?

'Yes, we kept running the business when father went. My father stood the market for years and years, and our Annie used to help him. 'Course in them days, it wasn't like it is today. As the market altered, we moved to the Peel Street side, and then later to the new market, so we've moved three times on the market over the years.'

I think the name of Southworth is always connected with tripe because it was so well known. So what was your Annie's married name, because she was a Southworth before?

'Cooke, Annie Cooke, she married Jim Cooke.'

Did you just do your three days

a week, then?

'Yes, but I stood Haslingden Market as well. We stood that for years on a Tuesday and Saturday market.'

And how did you find that at Haslingden—a lot quieter than Accrington perhaps?

'Sometimes, but it was a good market, and the people were very nice. But here in Accrington we had a happy stall. I mean Jim could tell a joke, and we used to have queues miles long, but no-one ever bickered or seemed to be in a hurry, because they were always entertained by Jim; he'd have them rolling with laughing with his jokes!'

He was a jolly man, wasn't he, as I remember him.

'Oh he really was—very jolly.'

So, we'll go back to the '30s when employment was getting a little bit better. Tripe was always a very reasonable, nourishing meal. What did you used to sell most of, can you remember?

'Well, it was always fatty seam.'

Because it was good for you?

'Yes, but we sold the lot; the dark tripe; the roll beef; the flat beef; cow heels; hundreds of trotters etc.'

What did they do with those, cook them in milk with onions?

'Yes, or with salt and vinegar on.'

They used to make cow heel pie didn't they?

'Oh yes, they were very popular in those days.'

But of course there were never

any U.C.P. tripe shops in Accrington, were there?

'There was one on Blackburn Road, you know, by Rosalyn Kenyon's hairdressers. It was the other half of the shop—near the Nag's Head it was.'

You see, I don't remember that; when did that close?

'Oh it closed a long time ago. Monk's had it for years.'

There was Eccles's tripe shop as well, wasn't there?

'Yes, and we were all good friends; there was never any bickering or anything. I mean there was Lawrence Wilson's egg stall; old Mr Wilson and his wife. She's living yet, she must be 80-odd. She could tell a story an' all.'

It probably wasn't as competitive then, but as you've come up over the years as well, the young people don't want fatty seam dow do they?

'No they don't, they're all after the honeycomb.'

And there is still a tripe factory in Blackburn, isn't there?

'Yes there is, but I don't know anything about it, oh there's a few, but it's a dying trade.'

Well, why do you think that is—maybe it's because the generation coming up want takeaways etc?

'Yes that's it, but you very seldom hear anybody mention tripe and they don't cook it, they have it just with salt and vinegar. It's dying out.'

And yet at one time you'd hear of businessmen having tripe after lunch, because it was good

for their stomach.

'Oh yes, it was always good for that.'

People like you and my father at 86 were brought up on tripe and lived to be a ripe old age on it.

'Yes I was only saying that this morning, and this lady says this generation won't be like us and live a long time. Yet they're all into health things at present aren't they?'

Going back again during the war, was the stall open late at night?

'Oh yes, we stood till 10 o'clock at night. Sometimes 11.'

There'd be gas lamps then, of course?

'Yes, I've seen my dad coming home at 11.30 many a time. He'd laugh because he'd be in his little wooden hut with this little lamp, and people did a lot of walking from Church coming back, and one chap used to say: 'Bob, there's about a dozen yet at back of me,' and he'd wait until they came on, It was amazing!'

It just shows the hours you put in, so eventually you closed your little shop—it was pulled down wasn't it?

'It was, but I can't say exactly when.'

Then you concentrated on your market stall?

'Yes, it was all market work after that.'

So what about your sister Annie and her husband Jim?

'Well, they were the main ones. Our Annie died in 1980, she was the last one as Jim had died in

1968. He was dead within 24 hours; thrombosis in his leg killed him. He wasn't very old, either. Twelve years after our Anne died.'

It seems a shame after all the hard work and many happy times you had.

'Yes, we've had some happy hours. It was the happiest time of my life, the market; even in Haslingden as well. I really enjoyed it. Everybody in those days were so friendly and sociable; we had everything really!'

Was it not as competitive as today?

'Oh no. We had everything going for us and worked together.'

Now, how about Haslingden Market itself, was that when it was in Deardengate?

'Oh yes, it was in the street. I moved out of the street when they opened the New Market inside, you see, and then they closed that.'

Deardengate now is all shops.

'Yes it is.'

They are nice people in Haslingden. Any characters you can remember particularly that came to your stall?

'No, I couldn't tell you any really. We had regulars, you know, people we knew for years and years, and we always knew their first names but never their last names. Even today I can meet people outside who'll say: 'hello', and I still don't know their last names! It's a long time ago to remember things. We just went on with our work. We worked very hard, we never had time to go and look at other stalls, in fact, you'd hardly time for your dinner!'

Were there queues all the time,

and did you sell black puddings as well?

'Oh, yes—home-made black puddings. My dad made them! We had a good black pudding trade.'

My mother used to come to your stall and buy them during the war. Were they not rationed during the war?

'Well, the dripping fat was. You'd to fight for that.'

I suppose tripe was a good supplement when there was only so much meat?

'Yes, it was, and we've turned some tripe out in our time. I worked down at the tripe shop during the war. My husband was called up for six years and I had two boys. When Derek, the baby, was born, my mother-in-law looked after him while I worked.'

That was the shop in Oak Street, wasn't it?

'Yes, then it was. When I was married I went to live in Richmond Hill Street. My husband came on leave and I used to stay at the shop and sleep there with the baby. Jack was born two years after but we were in Stanley Street then. Then I went to live in Blackpool with his mother, but that didn't work out.'

I'll bet you missed your tripe?

'Oh no. I travelled from Blackpool to work every Tuesday, Friday and Saturday, but I stayed overnight on Fridays and went back to Blackpool on Saturday night. My husband had a hairdressers' shop in Blackpool and then of course he got called-up for six years and I came back to Accrington and packed Blackpool up all together.'

Tommy isn't married, is he?

'He was, but he's a widower and he's no family to follow on.'

So who's running your Accrington stall now?

'Oh, it's not ours now, but Annie, my sister-in-law still goes up to the Haslingden market. Betty, is our Tom's housekeeper. Our Tom let her daughter have it, you see. We've nothing to do with it at all now.'

It's a shame, because it was a generation; father, grandfather, great-grandfather and so on.

'Yes, it was. It's amazing how things change. I've seen a big change and I don't think it's an improvement, myself, but this is progress, isn't it? There's nothing we can do about that!'

I was saying, were there a lot of Southworths?

'Oh yes! There was a big family of Southworths. When we lived in Oak Street, my father had bought that little lot of property in Grange Lane; all those cottages belonged to my dad. They've pulled them down now and we got nothing for them! My father was the youngest one and he was the one that got the business when grandad died. Well, there were four brothers besides and they disputed it; they said that because he was the youngest he shouldn't have had it, but grandma said that he was the only one capable of running it, as he had a good headpiece—so he took it over. He employed all the family and he put them in those cottages. There were about three of them in the cottages and one lived further down, just across the road from the shop. That was his brother, so they were all employed in the family, so he never made a lot of money. There wasn't a lot when he died because he looked after the family; he always did his best for them all. But that's all in the past, and, you see, they all had biggish families. Tommy Southworth, (that was one of the brothers) he was the next eldest. Well he worked at the tripe shop with my father. He was always the headman as he was a good tripe dresser. Now, Tommy had a lot of children, I've a lot of cousins—I couldn't remember them all!'

And yet if you look in the telephone book there's not a lot of Southworths?

'No, there's not.'

And it's an uncommon name, isn't it?

'There's more Southworths in Blackburn than there are in Accrington. They originally came from Blackburn. You know Samlesbury Hall, she was a Southworth.'

It's an unusual name isn't it? There was supposed to be a ghost too, wasn't there? It doesn't sound a Lancashire name.

'Oh yes. We've tried to go back to find out about it, but we couldn't. We got into a country place right up into the Ribble Valley and we couldn't get any further. They were farmers originally, but that's all I can tell you.'

Right. Now I'm going to speak to Elsie's husband who's called Syd Lambert. But you came from Blackpool, didn't you?

'Yes. I was from Blackpool but I was born in Rawtenstall. I was born in a pub! 'Bishop Blize Hotel', just near the market.'

I don't think that's there now, is it?

'Yes! It's there yet! I was there

until I was about seven years old then we went to Haslingden, and I was at grammar school there. Then we came out of public life and went into private life, so I was there till I was about fourteen. Then my parents took the 'Warners Arms' in Accrington. They were there, well, fourteen or fifteen years and then my dad died. My mother took it on and I helped her to run the cellar. I did all the cellar-work for my mum. Then I went into hairdressing. I went to 'Lawson and Kenyons' and I served my time there, in Blackburn Road.'

That was from the grammar school, was it, or did you change schools from Haslingden, or what?

'Yes. I went to St. James's for twelve months in Accrington, then I left at fourteen years old. When I was about fifteen or sixteen, my dad taught me how to do the cellar-work, and that's why I could take over when he died. Everybody used to have to muck in in those days. I know when I was at the Warners Arms, I used to scrub the floor on my hands and knees, because it was all lino then; very little carpeting. I used to have to scrub before I went to school and then, as I said before, I went to Lawsons and Kenyons for five years. That was an apprenticeship for hairdressing then.'

Did they do all hairdressing or did they do shaves etc, as well?

'Yes. They did all sorts—the lot— towels; shaves; singeing; shampooing; dyeing; etc.'

Oh, did they dye in those days then?

'Oh yes, but it wasn't like it is today. You had to be very careful because you couldn't just use it how you wanted to do. It was a very tricky job.'

Had you to learn to shave on a balloon before you shaved a person?

'Oh yes. I had to shave on a balloon and when you stopped bursting the balloon, you could shave a person. There used to be two or three people come in. I suppose they were 'guinea pigs' really. Practice blokes they were. We'd shave them; cut their hair; etc. Some people would come in every day for a shave.'

And how much was it for a shave then?

'It was 4d. It was dearer there than anywhere else, it was only 3d at other places.'

And did they still keep their custom?

'Oh yes, they got the businessmen and everything. They had a very high standard—what they call a first-class salon. It was 8d for a haircut—that was a big difference—it was 6d in other places. After I'd done my five years, I left and went to Blackpool, because after your apprenticeship, if they hadn't a job for you, you had to leave. Nine times out of ten they didn't.

Mr Lawson told me to go and get experience in different salons, so I went to Blackpool. In Blackpool I opened my own shop in Alfred Street. Then after I came out of the army, I came back to Accrington to my own shop in Stanley Street in about 1946. I stayed there for over thirty years until I retired about 11 years ago.

Well, a woman told me a tale about an aunt of hers whose husband had died. She went to the barber to ask how much it was for a shave:

'Tuppence,' he said.

'Well,' she said: 'I want thi ta cum t'heawse.'

'Well then, it's fourpence fer

thad,' he said.

'Well, it's like this, mi husband—he's laid out on a want 'im done proper like' she said.

'Alright then—id'll bi 1/6d fer thad' he replied.

'Oh well—dorned bother then, he's nod goin' anywheer special', she said and walked off.

Ther was one instance that happened with me in the salon, when I was in Stanley Street. There wer a fellow came in one night and he came in with a little boy. He sat down on a chair waiting and when it came their turn he says,

'I'll go first, because I've an errand to do after.'

So he sat down in the chair and I cut his hair and I think I shampooed him as well. Then he says,

'Will you cut the youngster's hair now?'

So he got the youngster in the chair and he says,

'I'll be back in half an hour.'

So I cuts the youngster's hair and then he sat down and I started doing the other people. It got about an hour and a half later and no-one had comeback for this little lad. I thought: 'That's funny.' So I says,

'How long will yer dad be before he comes for you?'

'Oh he's not mi dad,' sed lad, 'he picked me up in the street and asked if I'd like mi hair cut.'

So that was a funny incident. It wasn't a joke at the time but I can laugh at it now.'

It was a real pleasure to talk to both Elsie and Syd—two hard-working people who are still well-respected and remembered by many, many people in Accrington and surrounding districts.

||||||||||||||||||||||||||||||||||||||||||||||||||||||||

Mary Alice Hindle

Accrington and Acre, Haslingden

||||||||||||||||||||||||||||||||||||||||||||||||||||||||||||||||||||||||||||||||||||||||||||||||||||||||||||||||||||||||

Where were you born and bred?

'In Wigan. Mi mother was called Winstanley and her mother had eight children. Mi grandma was a 'knocker up' but when she went out to work mi mother did the 'knocking-up' for her. If she was frightened to go herself she would take me with her. I still had to go with mi mother when I started a full-time job as well. We went 'knocking-up' between four and four thirty early morning, then I went to mi own job. Colliers were the earliest to waken up. I would wait at the end of the lane whilst mi mother went up. She met a man there at the end of the lane and he was also a 'knocker-up'; and they walked down together. They carried a pit lamp because there were no street lights either, I can remember it very clearly.

We later came to Accrington because there was no work left in Wigan. I was thirteen when I went with mi mother as a 'knocker-up': we had to go up a long row. She went on one side and I did the other. One morning mi mother said she saw a man coming out of a garden on his hands and knees. He was out of one garden into another so mother told the other 'knocker up' (Harry) so he stopped to watch.

'You silly b-----', he said: 'That's not a man it's Ned Posslethwaite's donkey!'

Mi mother got tuppence off each customer every week which she had to give to grandma. It was her (grandma's) job really, but she wasn't always fit to do it.

I worked at Hazel Mill in Haslingden when I came over here from Wigan. The other children were too young to work, so we lived with mi grandma who had her own family as well. We had a three-mile walk to work, so four of us would meet up and walk together for a six thirty start. There was no transport at all then. We all wore shawls and carried our food for dinner in a wicker basket. We had to pass the railings of a park and we took turns at being first to pass this corner. It was my turn one morning when there was such a rattle on railings and we all started to run like mad. When we finally stopped and realised that it was 'mi stick' which had made the noise we were all breathless but we had a good laugh.'

Tell me about your childhood in Wigan

'I never had any really. We used to swing on a rope round the lamp posts and kick our clog irons on the pavements to make sparks. When we kicked the irons off we got a dammed good hiding. There was nothing but poverty and pawn shops then. We had a nice neighbour next door, though; they were Catholics and we were C. of E., and she had three children.

Mary Alice Hindle of Accrington

One Monday morning she came to mi mother's door with a parcel: 'take that to th' pop shop', she'd say: 'and pay me back at the week-end'. When the rent man was due to call, mother would get on her knees behind the door: 'I'll get below the letter box' she'd say; but he'd shout out: 'I know you're in,'—so you see what a life they had!

When I was coming up to the time for leaving school, I couldn't get a job, so mi mother said, 'Well Mary Alice, it doesn't matter if you can't get a job in th' factory, you'll have to go on th' pit top.'

There was a conveyor belt where the coal was tipped from the wagons as they came out of the cage. The girls had to sort out the various qualities of coal. I thought: 'Oh god, if I've to do that I'll dee.' However, mi dad came in one day and told me I'd to start work at a mill in Wigan. I wer paid three shillings and eightpence a week (app. 20p). I was helping to do the 'knocking-up' and then walking three miles to work and back for that pittance of a wage. It was

really hard work and we were 'only' poor. I married a man from Helmshore and came to live in Pilling Street, Acre.'

(Mary Alice showed Benita a pair of clogs, one of which her husband had clogged and the other she herself had done.)

'I still have the two lasts we used for making clogs with. One is very heavy, but I used the other, lighter one. When I worked at Acre Mill, I came on the tram to work and when I got off the tram on my first day there, I thought what a lovely place it was, but not as much as now. I worked in the card room.

I left Hazel Mill to go to Clough End, but because the two mills were amalgamated they wouldn't take me on. However, the manager suggested I find another job for a week or two, then perhaps I could start at another mill. This I did: but what a job it was; machining blankets in a dirty old room. I thought I'd never stick at it but I had no option so I carried on. A while later my former manager came in:

'Mary Alice,' he said, 'What are you doing here?' he says: 'You were one of our best workers in the card room.'

I said: 'Well, you should look after your good workers, then.'

He asked me to go back to the card room but I refused and I stayed in the sewing room.'

Did you go to Stonefold School?

'No, it was a nice school but they were 'clannish'. When it was 'walking day' the congregation had to pay for 'coffee and bun' to include 'them that 'ed nowt'. I were one that ' 'ed nowt'. One woman, a nice person, asked me had I paid my collection, I said 'No, an' I'm not doing 'cause I have no money, either.'

All my family were married at

Stonefold—it's a lovely church. My husband used to collect the newspapers. He got tuppence a week. He also brought tripe for the mayor. He told me once that he'd let the tripe fall in the 'slutch'. Seeing a pool of water further on he washed the tripe and the mayor never knew. My husband always said that it was a good thing customers never knew where the tripe had been. On one occasion it wer dropped in the cinders on the path and wer washed in the stream. I retired from work when I was sixty, and I've 'worked' like a damned fool ever since!'

Do you still go for walks?

'Yes, every morning at half past eight. I go for a walk around the tennis courts near the Coppice.

We had a good market in Haslingden and we bought a length of print which mi mother made into a blouse. That was the only way we could afford new clothes.

We had a Maypole every first of May and danced all along the streets. I was singled out to do the collecting bit.

Mi father liked a drink, but he was a good father, though he wouldn't let us be 'oyned' (put upon). We used to play in an area known as 'two fields'. I took all the local children with me. I took them up to mi auntie's as well. She was a real sanctimonious devil. She wasn't having all us lot in her house. (We were poor, you see.) We were bathed in all kinds of containers, from the 'dolly tub' to the big 'bread mug'.

I had two evacuees at one time. I'd one little girl of mi own, so two evacuees (girls) were brought to stay with me from Manchester. They were from a big family and they had some happy times with us. They were just like mi own children. I wanted them to go to work and send their wages to their own mother, but of course their own mother wanted them back.

Yes, I liked it at Acre, but it's nice now, wi mi daughter and I can walk around the Coppice [the local hill] every day!' (She even takes the dog around the Coppice three times a day as well!)

Mary Alice is a marvellous person, and looks as well and healthy as ever. She looks back with affection on her days as an 'apprentice knocker-up'.

‖‖‖‖‖‖‖‖‖‖‖‖‖‖‖‖‖‖‖‖‖‖‖‖‖‖‖‖‖‖‖‖‖‖‖‖‖‖‖

Syd Ashmead

Well-known band leader in Accrington

‖‖

Where were you born and bred, Syd?

'I was born in Lancaster in 1899, and came to Accrington in 1908. We came to Accrington because the iron works in Lancaster closed down. My father, along with one or two others walked it from Lancaster through the Trough of Bowland to Howard and Bullough's in Accrington.

My father started work at H. and

B.'s in 1908. I spent all my school days at Wesley Street United Methodists and started work 'half time' at Crossley Whewells' Heald Makers on Moscow Mill Street. I continued at Crossley Whewells when I left school and stayed there until I joined the 'young soldiers army' in 1917. Of course quite a lot happened before then.'

Tell us about it Syd, please.

'Well, recently there's been a lot of publicity when the Accrington Conservative Club closed down. Amongst all the people who were mentioned, I could have gone back further in memory than any of them. The first time I played for dancing at 'The Con' was in 1912. I was only twelve years old, but already a member of Howard and Bullough's Military Band. The whole band used to play at the Conservative Club—mostly it was old-time dancing—lancers, waltzes, barn dances, to name but a few. At this time in Accrington there were two military bands and three brass bands. There was Howard and Bullough's Military Band, Accrington Old Band, Church and Oswaldtwistle Prize Band and Clayton-le-Moors Prize Band.

During my life I've played with all of them. I was in the forces and later went with the army of occupation to Germany in 1919.

We lived on Hagg Lane, Hyndburn Road, at this time. During the war, women had to take over the men's jobs and so I couldn't get work. My father at this time was foreman in the Dressing Department at Howard and Bulloughs and I eventually got a job there as a labourer. It was 1920 when I came back from Germany and it was 1922 before I got work. I married in 1925 and went to live in Fielding Lane, Oswaldtwistle. When I bought that house I paid £150 for it, but I had to move because my wife was diabetic. We moved to Green Haworth on the

doctor's advice for the fresh air. We had to carry every bucket of water from the well at the end of Cross Edge. My brothers gutted the cottage and found that the bedroom floors consisted of two layers of flags with soil in between. We carried those paving stones out of the house and got the council workers to take them away. We boarded the floors but still had no water laid on, or electricity either. We did get gas, though.

My wife died in 1929, so I came back home. During that time my wife's brother, Cecil Dunnochie, was organist at St. Paul's Church on Catlow Hall Street and between us we formed a little dance band. We played the first time as a band at the Conservative Club in Rhyddings Street, Oswaldtwistle, with a four-piece band. We continued with the band for a few years as the Ritz Orchestra and we gradually increased the number of players. After the war, Councillor William Metcalfe organised a Memorial Ball in Oswaldtwistle. This became an annual event and was considered a 'plum' engagement for the band. The booking we got for this dance really started us with a bigger orchestra. Later Cecil left the band so I had to get another pianist. I opened at Church Conservative Club when it was newly built.

There used to be a well-known music firm in Accrington called 'J. S. Haworth—Ritz Orchestra', it was a way of advertising the music firm. Our bookings increased and we became a ten-piece band. We played at Blackburn, Preston, Morecambe—in fact all over the place! I played at the majority of the private dances at 'The Con' but Holgates were the resident band. The popular band in the district when I first started was 'Billy Rushton's'. At this time all Accrington musicians had to be members of the musicians' union. I also played in the pit orchestra at Accrington Theatre—(Princes' in

Edgar Street). When the Second World War started, I was still working at Howard and Bulloughs on the staff. The band was stll flourishing and became the works' band from 1940 to 1964. I was resident band at the Ritz Ballroom in Accrington. I retired from H. & B.'s in 1964 and I left the band as well so it was all finished. We broadcast from Howard and Bullough's and also from Manchester. It was a 'Homes Exhibition' and the BBC did a broadcast from there and we were chosen as the accompanying band. I have recordings of all these events. I was trumpet player and when I retired Bob Watmough was my pianist. He eventually took over the band at the Ritz and is still playing locally.'

Dancing has changed a lot, over the years, hasn't it Syd?

'I don't think people would like to hear my views on that, but I know the people I meet in town still say: 'Syd Ashmead, I've had some good times dancing to your band, I wish you were back again.'

I used to do Sunday concerts for charity. A councillor called Sydney Tetlow used to run dances for the 'Clog Fund' and I used to provide the band for those. Then for many years a chap called Jack Parmley, who was a keen supporter of the Accrington Cricket Club, used to engage me to play at Sunday night concerts for the various funds. We played for the nurses at Blackburn Infirmary, and for charity, as well.'

Tell us about the Hippodrome.

'It's rather strange, but I remember as an eight-year-old boy standing in the front garden of the house where we used to live, in Charter Street, and watching the old Hippodrome burn down. It was a wooden building then, and I saw the new one being built, and I went to play there—I've played all

over. My father played the cornet and he taught me to play the instruments. My father formed the band for the Accrington Pals Battalion, as well. Colonel Lipman came and he expressed a desire for a brass band. The greater part of the instruments came from Howard and Bulloughs because their band had to break up. The instruments were bought out of store and passed to the 'Pals'—that's how the band was formed. In 1915 my father was drum major of the band and led the procession from Church Commercial through Accrington in a 'grand march' through the town. Father was also a 'crack shot' and eventually had to leave the battalion and train recruits in musketry. I often played at the reunion of the 'Pals' after the war, at Argyle Street Barracks. I used to have a band at Hodder Bridge Hotel. We played for the afternoon tea dances and on a Sunday evening it was a very popular place.'

Did you play in the local parks?

'I had the distinction, as a boy of twelve, of playing the tenor horn, solo, from *Poet and Peasant* in Oak Hill Park. This piece is a good test of the ability of a musician. Yes, I played in the various parks for many years. I've played at Mercer Hall, Great Harwood for dancing till 2 a.m., then walked it back over the 'switchback' to Fielding Lane, Oswaldtwistle and then started work at Howard and Bullough's at 7.30 a.m. until 5.30 p.m.'

You must have been fit.

'Well, it's rather strange, but until I went in the army, I was never really well. I had an operation on mi lungs when I was four years old. I was bronchial up to going in the army. I used to put a ten-piece band on, and a vocalist at 'Accrington Con' and I had to get all the players home afterwards,

including transport, for £25. Today they get £50 per man. But it was all very enjoyable otherwise we wouldn't have done it.'

Syd lives very happily in retirement and he and his wife Hilda celebrated their Golden Wedding not long since. He has given many Accrington people a lot of pleasure and they all remember him with affection.

Unfortunately, Syd has since died but I am so glad that I was able to speak to him.

||||||||||||||||||||||||||||||||||||||||||||||||||||||||||

St John's Church, Accrington

Lancashire's Mighty Mills

Those mighty mills with chimneys rising high,
Outlined in the orange evening sky,
Pointing upwards—belching smoke each hour
Lancashire's answer to the Eiffel Tower?
Their solemn grandeur braved all winds and rains
Guardians of those ancient family names—
Hargreaves; Arkwrights; Cromptons—long forgotten
But once synonymous with England's cotton.
Behold the pulsing arteries of the trade
Stand empty now, forgotten and decayed.
The staff of life—the weaver's bread and butter,
Those mighty mills reduced to worthless clutter.
What dreams they represented—hopes and fears,
Eternal benefactors down the years.
Their sad demise from favour—cotton's death
As chimney after chimney drew last breath.
The spinners and the weavers sent in flight
To other climes with no chimneys in sight.
The towns are silent, lonely as the hills;
Empty now without their mighty mills.
Forgotten now the heritage sublime—
The mills are gone, Lancashire's in decline.
Looms and shuttles relegated to the past,
Long gone the clogs and shawls and cobbler's last.
And yet there still remains a legacy
To show how proud Lancashire used to be,
The chimneys black of those proud, mighty mills
Still stand defiant 'neath the Pennine hills.

Benita Moore

Jack Walmsley

Clogmaker, from Baxenden

Where were you born and bred, Jack?

'Up 'Bash' [Baxenden]. I went to school there and to the grammar school which I left when I was fifteen. Our clogger's shop was getting too much for mi dad and there was much unemployment. I couldn't get a job so I went to work with mi dad. He learnt his trade at the Accrington Co-op. At first he worked in a mill during the day, and after he'd had his tea went down to the shop in Oak Street to learn about clogging.'

I believe that your father was deaf and dumb?

'Yes. His customers had to write on a slate to explain what they wanted. If he'd been normal he could have 'gone a long way'; he was a very clever man, and a very good clogger—everyone knew that. He soon learnt how to make very good clogs.'

What do you remember about your early days as a clogger?

'Well, just mending shoes and clogs mostly. I preferred to make clogs, it was a more skilled trade. I made the soles from pieces of wood, and we made different sizes. Then we got the skins to make the uppers, and we got them in Accrington. The skins were tanned at a big place in Carlisle; they were a very fine cow hide. The machines were so good they could cut the skins in two quite easily. We cut the soles to size, then hollowed out for the foot. The upper was then cut and shaped to the sole. We then nailed irons on the bottom, much to the delight of children who used to kick the iron on the ground to make the sparks fly. The clog irons were made at Hebden Bridge and they were very strong.'

What hours did you work then?

'Mi dad started at six a.m.— sometimes 5.30 a.m. and seldom finished before 8 p.m. When I started work it was from 8.30 a.m. until ten or eleven at night. A pair of clogs was made for six or seven shillings (35p). Farmers' lace-up clogs cost about one pound. They took a lot of time to shape and stitch and iron. All the mill workers wore clogs which they had to buy themselves, no firms supplied them. It's a pity the wearing of clogs has gone as nothing was better for the feet providing the soles were properly shaped. I would never have put my son in the trade though, there was no money in it and a lot of skilled work. There were any amount of cloggers, you know, at one time. There was one at the bottom of Union Street in Accrington, one in Abbey Street, and another on Bull Bridge, and they all managed to scrape a living of some sort, although some gave it up.

Colliers came for clogs as well. They worked at Broad Oak pit—it was a shaft from the hillside which produced coal for Broad Oak Print Works, and textiles.

When the clog trade ended I kept on with the shoe repairing, but I always preferred to make clogs though—it was more satisfying. When they were finished and polished with brass nails all round the edge of the sole, they were a work of art. I worked full-time until I was seventy then part-time for another five years.'

Why did the clog trade die?

'Well they were looked upon as footwear for the poor so as people became more affluent they started to wear shoes.'

Since I spoke to him, though, sadly Jack has died. He did actually have a shop in Baxenden until 1975, and all the local people knew him for his good workmanship. He's fondly remembered as 'Baxenden's last clogger' and deserves to be given credit for his hard work over the years and his devotion to producing quality clogs.

Rose Mill decorated for the Coronation in 1911

Henry Williams

Owner of Woods Tobacconists in Accrington

'I was born in Garbett Street, Accrington, and came to work for Woods Tobacconists when I left school. The business was started in 1875 by the two brothers, Colin and Major Wood. The business used to be on Piccadilly, facing the Market Hall, then on the corner of Blackburn Road in the 1920s, but came to these premises, on Union Street, which used to be the warehouse, in the 1930s. We are still in Union Street and I took over in the 1960s after the partnership of the Woods' brothers ended. We sold more loose tobacco in the old days and twist. Along with the *Accrington Observer* we arranged to despatch cigarettes to the forces in the 1940s which was much appreciated by our men.

We had a big wholesale trade supplying shops in all the surrounding districts and I used to collect 'bad debts'. I got 2½ per cent commission and I often had to put my foot in the door to get sixpence (2½p). We sold a lot of snuff and we could tell snuff-takers because it was all over their waistcoats. 'Owd Bob's Twist' was our trade mark and we sold over two hundredweight a week, it was made by Cowells of Liverpool. The miners used to chew plugs of tobacco. It was said that the tobacco used to be wrapped around the neck and cut to size rather than weighed, as they could gauge the exact amount after years of experience. A clay pipe was given free with their measure of tobacco. We still sell twist, as well as cigarettes. Twist was eight pence an ounce when I started, it's now £1.70. We still sell a lot of loose tobacco and now have a sale for brassware and 'Pendelton' ware from Burnley. We've also walking sticks and pipes.

A man called Ben Ainsworth who worked at the back of the

Market Hall did our pipe and lighter repairs. A Dunhill pipe cost 12/6d in the old days; a cheaper one was 2/6d (25p). We had one or two Irish ladies in the past who smoked twist in a clay pipe and the Irish navvies smoked clay pipes as well. These men built the 'Cock Bridge' over the river Hyndburn. These old clay pipes are still being discovered on the sites of the old building sites where the men worked. Snuff is made from pipe tobacco, with the addition of eucalyptus and other flavours. It was claimed that 'snuff takers' didn't contract influenza or bad colds because the snuff kept the lungs and nose clear. Taken in moderation it was a good thing. After the war, cigarettes were still rationed and we could sell all our week's allocation on a Wednesday morning alone. Woodbines wer 2/4d for twenty and they were one of the most popular brands. Tobacco sales are dropping but I don't think smoking will be cut out all together.

There are many kinds of pipes; Cherry Wood, Briar, Meerschaum pipes from Turkey etc. Corn Cob pipes come from America but we sell Briar pipes more than any other. We also stock 'Sherlock Holmes' pipes which are still quite popular. Accrington Stanley cost us a lot of pipes. The men bought them on the way to the match and allowed them to burn too fiercely in their exitement, thus burning a hole in the bowl, so on the Monday morning more pipes were bought to replace the burnt ones. When Accrington Stanley disappeared, it cost us a lot of pipe sales and we now have side-lines to help our sales. We still keep quite a variety of loose tobaccos, though which are quite popular. The old family businesses like these are dying out though, which is a pity.'

twist and all kinds of other interesting products met you as you entered the front door. A gleaming array of bottles, snuff tins, cigarettes, brasses and many other products made the shop very attractive to even the non-smoker. But most of all I was delighted to see the good selection of pipes and walking sticks which Harry

It was a delight to talk to Harry in his shop. The smell of tobacco, snuff,

still prides himself on keeping.
'Woods Tobacconists' in Union Street, Accrington is the best little shop of its kind in the area and I hope Harry Williams continues to maintain it for many more years to come.

IIIIIIIIIIIIIIIIIIIIIIIIIIIIIIIIIIIIIIIIIIIIIIIIIIIIIII

Jacksons' Lamp

I went an errand t'other day, on't street where I were born,
They're pulling all th'owd buildings down, it all looked so forlorn!
But it's all in't name o'progress, at least that's what they say,
For t'powers that be have said we need a brand new motorway.
They've flattened little toffee shop where we used to spend our pennies,
I never did know th'owners name—we always called it 'Jennies'
I've had many a stick of spanish, and bags of kali too,
She used to sell gob-stoppers, striped green and red and blue.
It's there we played at 'opscotch, and top and whip and all,
And t'lads 'ud play at marbles, and rounders wi' a ball.
But t'best game for us lasses, while t'mothers 'ad a camp,
Were to throw our straw ropes over, and swing on Jacksons' lamp.
Now some o'you that's younger won't know just what I mean,
By throwin' t'straw ropes over, I bet you've never seen
T'straw ropes that came all plaited round t'wooden crates o'fruit,
Eh! They were tough and strong alright, but what's more—free to boot.
Th'owd gas lamps as they 'ad then 'ad an arm that stuck straight out,
And on a summer evening sometimes there'd be a shout—
'They've got straw rope at Nellies'—that being t'green-grocers shop,
Eh, you wouldn't see our heels for dust, we'd run and never stop.
Till we landed there all breathless, bright eyed and full of 'ope,
That Nellie 'adn't parted with her last long length of rope.
Then back again to throw it right over th'iron bar,
Then tie a knot in t'bottom, and swing out so far.
It were up and up and higher, and round and round and round,
Then t'other way, unwinding, and your feet back down on't ground.
Eh! It were Jacksons' lamp alright, it stood outside their door,
And you daren't fall out with Jacksons', you'd not swing that night for sure.
It fairly takes me back a bit, and just 'tween you and me,
Although I'm what they call an active O.A.P.,
If you'd give me an old straw rope, and a lamp with an iron bar,
I'd soon show you lot how it's done, a swinging out so far.
It would be up and up and higher, and round and round and round,
Then—t'other way, unwinding and mi' feet back down on't ground.

Frances Dooley

IIIIIIIIIIIIIIIIIIIIIIIIIIIIIIIIIIIIIIIIIIIIIIIIIIIIIIIIIIIIIIIIIIIIIIIIIIIIIIIIIII

Irene Westell

(née Buller), of Accrington

||||||||||||||||||||||||||||||||||||||||||||||||||||||||||||||||||||||||||||||||||||||||||||||||||||||||||||||||||||||||||||||||||||||||||||

IRENE lives at Clarendon Street and she told me many interesting things about the Black Abbey area. She's not all that old but she has a good memory.

'Well, I'm nearly 65 actually and I was born in Birtwistle Street, just off Abbey Street more or less across from Black Abbey. I lived there until I was seven years old, then we moved to Spencer Street, which is near here. Then we moved down into Stanley Street then Lodge Street and from there I got married. But my childhood down in Birtwistle Street was very interesting. At the bottom of the street, in the last house was a man called Mr Barnes, but he was always known as 'Bunny'. He used to sell second-hand furniture which he used to put out on the pavement. He had deformed feet and he wore like a leather casing round them. He and his wife and children lived there and I remember across from there was the Oak Tree Inn and across the road in Abbey Street was the Red Lion Inn, which is still there but under another name. That was at the top of Black Abbey and I remember there was an iron road between the top of Black Abbey to Plantation Street in my childhood days.'

An iron road, what was that?

'Well, they were like iron blocks with knobbles on them but they were very slippy in winter and the horses used to slip on them. Most deliveries in those days were done by horse and cart and I remember three girls being knocked down by a coal wagon and two of them died. Soon after that they took them up and made the road safer.'

You know, that iron road perhaps went up to Arden Hall—I did it?

'No, it only went from Black Abbey and just past that stretch of shops to the bottom of Plantation Street. Then there was 'Briggs' Yard' next to the Oak Tree Inn. Through there were some little houses; one up some steps, and when we were children; Hargreaves Street, where New Jerusalem Church was at the time, had a long wall attached to the Church and you could look over the wall into Briggs' Yard. An old lady used to come out onto these steps and we thought she was a witch. I know we used to call her 'Mother Shipton' anyway.'

Which school were you at?

'Till I was seven, I went to St. Paul's and then I moved to St. Anne's because actually my mother was a Catholic and she wanted me in her religion. But St. Paul's is still called Benjamin Hargreaves School

sometimes and all my brothers went and I had a sister who died twelve months before I was born; she went there too! I know in Black Abbey we used to love going in Saul's shop, and up the stairs and looking under the bannister that went round, and the money going through the air on wires in little tin cans. They sold all sorts; but upstairs it was always drapery. I can remember, though—this might sound strange as I was only in a pram, but you know how some things stick in a child's mind? Well mi mother took mi down Oak Street to watch a wedding that was at the Church at the corner there of Bank Street and Oak Street. Across from the church, on Oak Street, there was an 'entry', there was like houses and shops around, and up this 'entry' there used to be a basketmakers' place. He used to repair baskets fer weavers who took their lunches to work in these baskets. I can remember mi mother had pushed me into this 'entry' (whether it was raining or what I don't know). Anyway, she left me in this 'entry' while she went to watch this wedding, who was a girl she used to work with when she wer weaving. There was the Co-op butchers and the Co-op cloggers there, and I can remember having mi clogs mended there when I was little. They used to pull yer leg and mi name was Buller then and I can remember him (the clogger) saying one day to somebody in the shop: 'Do you know her father's General Buller?' and I really thought he was!

In those days you could go errands without fear of crossing the roads because there wasn't as much traffic etc.'

Were the trams not running then?

'Yes. They used to go up to Haslingden but they weren't fast like a car. There wcre quite a few accidents on Abbey Street. Co-op cloggers were once next door to the Red Lion, down some steps, where there was a fire once. At the corner of Oak Street was the Co-op confectioners and they had a cafe and if they'd had a wedding on or a funeral and there was anything left they'd put out for sale into the shop. They did their own baking always. There was a bakers there then, the confectioners then around the corner was the cloggers, then the grocers, then the butchers and then there was a door leading into the bakehouse. I can remember going down there once when I worked for the Co-op; they'd run out of bread and they'd sent me down fer some.'

What was this about a man who used to come with roundabouts in the streets?

'Yes, I've seen them come with a roundabout on the back of a horse and cart. Thery'd be about five or six swing roundabouts and I think it was about a halfpenny a ride. And an ice-cream man and hot peas used to come as well. The ice-cream man was called Louis Brown. He was an Italian really and he had a big moustache and a check waistcoat with a gold fob watch. He was very clean with a big white apron and he'd push a hand cart and it was lovely ice-cream. I remember up Chapel Street one day, at the back of the New Jerusalem Church and the Sunday School, an organ grinder came round with a monkey and we went to watch him. The monkey ran up the drainpipe and he couldn't get it down at one time.'

What was that about some bears in the area?

'Oh that was some relation of Louis Brown. He used to take lodgers in and my uncle used to lodge with them and I suppose when the travelling shows and fairs came and they took them in, some would

come with these bears. My uncle said that while he was there they had a bear in the cellar; they weren't really fierce. I remember when they used to come selling coal on the carts, they used to shout: 'Black Diamonds. So much a bag.' About 1/6d a bag I think then.'

Of course you'd be young during the '30s?

'Yes, I was born in 1924.'

What was that story about your auntie and the tea towel?

'Well, if mi mother wasn't so well, mi auntie would take me up to her house, and she lived at the top of Spencer Street. Me and mi cousin used to go up the Coppice with some friends and we'd take sandwiches and lemonade or something like that. Mi auntie would say that when our tea was ready she'd stand at the door and wave a pot-towel which meant that we'd to come home fer our tea. First time I ever had prunes was at mi aunties and I didn't like them and when I went home I said to mi mother: 'We had some things with cold tea on them.' I thought she'd put cold tea on them but it wer the juice.'

Didn't you say that someone had told you there was a passage under Balck Abbey?

'Oh yes. That was when the houses were built round and that tunnel was there. The old man who used to live next door to me, Mr Mulhall, he was a sanitary inspector for the town. He said there was a tunnel but you could only go part way up and then it was blocked up. There must have been a fall or something, but it was said it went right up through to Whalley Abbey. I know I did read somewhere—I think it was in a book, *The Old Homesteads of Accrington*, that there

was a treaty signed by the monks of Whalley Abbey where the Red Lion stands now. There's walls at the back of there, down in the cellar, which were probably part of the tunnel. Of course, it was once a coaching house to Manchester.'

Well there was supposed to have been an abbey there once.

'Well, that was where it got its name Black Abbey from (I think)—Abbey Street as well.'

And didn't Moseley's Bakery used to be down there as well?

'Oh yes, down Jacob Street. I know we used to play at Black Abbey and I used to think that the back of the Church in Oak Street came on to Black Abbey and I thought perhaps that wall was part of Black Abbey as well.'

So what was your first job when you left school?

'I did go three days to learn hairdressing and then I went to the leatherworks at the bottom of Water Street. Walmsleys, it was called. I was there until I was sixteen and then went to work for the Co-op in the grocery. Then when I was eighteen, during the war, I had to go on war work and I was sent to Mullards at Blackburn.'

What did you make in the leatherworks?

'They used to make straps fer machinery and we made a kind of hook made into a fastener which fastened these belts round the machines. We used to set a press up for these hooks to be welded to clamp the ends of the belts together to hold it.'

What happened after the war?

'Well, when I left Mullards I went to work at Broad Oak and I was there until I got married. I did all sorts of jobs, but they were doing some sort of badges fer uniforms. Cutting badges out, which I started on, but we got moved about a lot.'

My dad worked at Steiners during the war.

'My uncle was a shop steward at Steiners and he's still living, he'll be 94 in September!' (Steiners was a well-known printworks at Church.)

So what about the market, can you remember anything about that when you were a little girl?

'One thing I remember about Accrington Market is, at the corner of Peel Street and Blackburn Road there used to be 'The Banana King' (Fureys). He used to be open until 10 o'clock and all the market was open till 10 o'clock in those days. He used to shout: 'Canary Bananas'—they must have been special in those days. He never sold anything else only these Canary Bananas—they were very small. During the war they enclosed it all in wood. During the war, when I worked for the Co-op, we were sometimes sent down to the market to help on the stall there. We'd be coming out about 10 o'clock when it closed and it was so dark we could hardly find our way home. It wasn't really safe though because anybody could have been hiding in the passages.'

Well, where was this stall of the Co-op's?

'It was where Lightfoots is now, that was the Co-op stall then. I know the manager was an officer in the Home Guard but I can't remember his name. The girls were to replace the men that were called up fer National Service.'

You have quite a good memory, haven't you, and of course this

area, which was Birtwistle Street, it's all changed hasn't it?

'I know. I remember when I was a child it was so hot—we'd run about in our bare feet on the pavement which was red-hot. That must have been in the late 1920s and we used to get real thunderstorms then. Where Plantation Square is now, there used to be some little cottages, and some girls who went to the same school as me lived there. Their house was struck by lightning and it was flooded out. A little boy nearly drowned and they found him under the table in the water. In fact they're still living and they live in Bold Street.'

Was the Coppice different then? (N.B. The Coppice is a green hill at the top of Avenue Parade in Accrington much loved by local people.)

'Oh yes. It was all open fields and there was 'Johnny's Pad'. That was a path that cut across the top of Bold Street. There were 'pens' where those bungalows are now and the path cut across the back of those pens. 'Johnny's Pad' was called after Johnny Riddihough, (I think). He was a farmer. I know one of my brothers used to take milk round for him. What they called: 'Kitting Milk' They had Kit measures and it would be poured into somebody's jug. That's a long time ago.'

Did you ever go dancing in your teens?

'Not really. The only time I went dancing was when I was going to school. We used to go to Madame Butterworths on Knowlmere Street, and it was known as: 'Madame Butts'. We used to go Friday night and Saturday morning and it cost us 9d. We learnt ballroom dancing and tap dancing. There was Mrs. Butterworth, a little, stout woman; her daughter who was very tall and

they taught us ballroom dancing. The son, who was slightly deformed, used to play the piano. We used to love going there. About two or three years ago my husband's uncle took about eight of us out fer a celebration meal, and he said: 'I'm taking you somewhere else after', and we landed up at Madame Butterworths. When I walked in -it looked so tiny as to how I remembered it when I was a child; then it had looked big. It seemed so small and it really brought some memories back because I hadn't been back since I was a little girl. I'll tell you about the police station when that was being built. I remember going up there with a boy I used to play with. We'd be about six or seven years old. His father worked on the building site and we used to take his lunch up in a red handkerchief. The old police station was down Union Street. I used to get lost and I'd go up in the Union Street Police Station and wait fer mother. I seem to remember it was painted green and I couldn't have been very old, about three or four years old, but I remember it vividly.' (The old police station was where Barclays Bank is now in Union Street.)

At one time they seemed to paint everything dark green. Public toilets etc.

'I remember the toilets in Dutton Street. My mother used to live near the new police station in Manchester Road. There used to be two or three little streets and she lived at the bottom of there.'

Is that where the Law Courts are?

'I couldn't tell you the name of the streets but that's where the Wesley Church was. I remember that was there—then it was pulled-down. I have a book somewhere that was printed especially for that church and it's a recipe book and members of the church put recipes in this book, I suppose to raise money for the church. In Hargreaves Street, where the New Jerusalem Sunday School was, the church was in Abbey Street and the back of the church came into Hargreaves Street and the Sunday School was across the road. It was a lovely Sunday School. I know one Sunday mi mother couldn't find me and they found me in the Sunday School singing round the piano and I was dirty because I'd been playing out and I'd followed the children into the school. They were very good with me and even though I turned Catholic when I was seven years old, every year I got a birthday card signed by the Rev. Edge right up to being twenty-one. Wherever I moved to, they must have found out where I was and sent a card.'

Really though, you've moved a lot and it's always been in the same area and now you're back where you started.

'I was talking to a woman in the bungalows and she lived down there in Birtwistle Street. There was a big family of them in them houses and she said when she got married she was living in Church, in a flat and now they've put her in one of these bungalows on Plantation Square. She said it's lovely where she is and it feels like she's come home again. And that's how I feel now. Where the football field is now at the bottom of the Coppice going up to Arden Hall— that wasn't a flat field. At the back of the garages it's sloped down like it does now from these 'pens' to the lodge. There was a stream which ran down the bottom of there where we used to play. We'd run down the hill and step across the water on the stones. That stream came down from a dyeworks at the top of the lane, past Arden Hall. Sometimes the stream would be blue, sometimes

red and different colours. I had a cousin who used to work there years ago and the people were still living in Arden Hall then. Afterwards it was made into a little park.'

Well, this area, Plantation Street, has quite a lot of history attached to it. The church would be there, wouldn't it?

'Oh yes, me and mi brothers went. Mi oldest brother's eighty years old.'

You were saying about rag and bone chaps that used to come through.

'Yes they did and we used to get donkey stones off them or pennies if we'd no pennies to go to the Palace pictures. I loved the picture Palace, it used to be 2d!'

Oh yes. That's where Melia's was. It's a miniature market now.

'Mi mother used to give me 3d and we'd go down to Woolworth's and buy a bag of broken biscuits and then sit in the pictures eating them all afternoon.'

Woolworth's was then on Piccadilly, facing the Town Hall wasn't it?

'Yes, 3d and 6d stores. At Christmas we used to go up the flight of steps on your left. At the top there'd be Father Christmas and parcels would be 6d. A pink one for girls and a blue one for boys. I always remember I once got a toy telephone in one and it was one of those old time things that hooked on. My childhood had some really good days and even today I still bump into friends from long ago and it's like meeting long, lost sisters, though there's not as many of us now. There's Lucy round the corner—she used to live

down Plantation Street, at the corner of Elephant Street and Plantation Street. Her father was a barber. I can't remember his name but she's called Lucy Feeley now. She married a Feeley. I know next to her father's shop was a grocers shop and across the road was a lodging house, at the corner of the King's Arms.

There used to be a barbers up Higher Pitt Street; that was off Plantation Street. There was Hilda Pearson's at the corner of Plantation Street—she sold greengrocery and she'd sell cut fruit cheaply.

Across the road from there, at the bottom of Higher Pitt Street and Plantation Street, was 'Mother Gumms'; she sold toffee but she was a sort of herbalist as well. It was very interesting.'

How big of a family had you?

'I'd two brothers. My oldest brother was a twin but my sister died when she was fourteen.

Then I was born twelve months after that. My eldest brother's eighty and the other is seventy-six now.'

There's quite a gap between you, isn't there?

'Yes there's eleven years between my youngest brother. I know mi mother used to nurse me a lot in them days. I'd measles, scarlet fever; I had that three times! I had it when I was twenty-one.'

At one time it was said that there could be disease through cotton, is that correct?

'Yes. Well they used to get a lot of cotton from Egypt in those days. I hadn't a bad childhood really; the friends I had then, they're still friends now. There's one I have and we were born in the same street and we went to the same school at St. Anne's, and when I see her she makes a right fuss!'

Of course, at one time the families all tended to live in the same street, didn't they?

'Yes. Mi auntie always looked after me if mi mother wasn't so well. She was mi mother's sister and she had four daughters and two sons and she adopted a girl when she was fourteen, whose mother had died. She went to school with one of her daughters and she always called mi: Auntie 'Mother' all through the years. Then mi auntie moved to Blackpool and I used to go a lot at weekends and take mi mother along. My parents separated when I was a child. That's how I became a Catholic at seven years old. Mi mother came from an Irish family and mi father was English.'

You were going to tell me about someone you knew.

'Oh yes. A person who lived up Hargreaves Street. We used to call her 'Blind Polly'. She was small and stout and of course blind and she always wore a hat a bit like a nurse's hat. She always wore black; a black skirt; black stockings and lace-up boots; little round, pale face she had. If we saw her coming down the street we'd ask if we could take her across the road. She lived at the top of Hargreaves Street, there were five houses, I think, there—just higher up than the Jerusalem Sunday School.'

A lot of these characters need remembering, don't they?

'Yes, they do. There used to be a man who was at the lodging house at the top of Pitt Street. They called him 'Teddy'. He was a short man and he reminded you of a teddy bear in a way and he used to push a hand-cart—I think he sold firewood or something like that. He was a harmless, little man but he's a person you'd remember.'

Well, there used to be rag and bone men. Do you remember anyone coming round selling muffins?

'Oh yes. We had a 'muffin man'; he came from either Rishton or Great Harwood and he'd sell oat-cakes and mi mother would hang them on the rack. Don't ask me why! Sometimes she'd tell him she had no money so she didn't want any but he'd still leave them and say she could pay for them later. He would carry his basket on his head and I remember him well.'

Irene has four sons of her own now and she was fascinating to talk to. Not many people remember the Plantation Street and Black Abbey area like she does.

The Duckett Brothers

from Oswaldtwistle

FRANCIS and Tom Duckett are two very well-known brothers in Oswaldtwistle. They've had a long connection with the building trade and are renowned for first-class work. They've also had a very interesting childhood, their step-grandfather being the proud owner of waggonettes, which were in great demand for funerals, parties, or simply trips out. They could remember these jaunts quite clearly and I was very happy to speak to them both.

Francis

Where were you born, Francis?

'No. 1, Fielding Lane, Oswald-twistle, near here where I live now.'

Tell me about the waggonettes your step-grandfather had.

'He used to keep them at the bottom of Fielding Lane, behind Catlow Hall Street. There was also a funeral hearse, all glass, and my father used to drive it.

The horses wore big, black plumes on their heads for funerals. 'Smith' was the trading name, (the name of my step-grandfather) and we also had a pony and trap which my father used to take us out in when he could. The waggonettes were elevated, so we had to use steps at the back to get to the wooden seats. The waggonettes took people out to the Ribble Valley, much as coaches do today. At one time they were used as public transport between Oswaldtwistle and Accrington and were very popular. My step-grandfather was called Ernest Smith!"

Which school did you go to?

Ernest Smith's Funeral Wagonette in Oswaldtwistle, 1912.
(Ernest Smith was the step-grandfather of the Duckett brothers)

'St. Mary's R.C., Oswaldtwistle. I left at fourteen and went to work in 'Bridges' ironmongers in Market Street, Church, now long gone, but a lot of people still remember it being there. After three years I was transferred to the main shop at Accrington at the corner of Church Street. I was there until I had to go into the forces in 1939. I was taken prisoner at Boulogne and sent to a prisoner of war camp in East Prussia, Stalag X2A and Stalag SXB. It wasn't too bad for me because I never stayed in the camp. I had to go out on working parties all over East Prussia, working on farms. Anyone below a sergeant had to work and we also got more food while working. The basic ration consisted of half a loaf of dark bread plus a bit of jam and margarine and erzatz coffee each day. Sometimes we worked in a food factory where we could always do a bit of back-handing. I worked

in cheese factories, a sugar-beet factory and a sawmill. After about two years Red Cross parcels started to arrive. A lot of this food went to the Germans in the front line but we got our quota! The parcels came from England, Canada, America and Australia. This extra food kept us going; without it, I'm sure a lot of us wouldn't have come back. In the beginning we got one parcel between two men but later we got one each. I was in these working camps until January 1945; that was when the trouble started.

I was on the 1,500km march from east to west. I can't remember how I survived. I don't even remember eating! I know I must have had something but there was no Red Cross; just nothing! It was a very bad winter and I know when I came home, mi big toes were so frost-bitten that I could put matches through 'em. I was lucky, I was always skinny; it was the big

men that suffered most on the march; it appeared they needed more to sustain them. I never took my clothes off from January 29th 1945 until May 3rd 1945. We ended up on the west coast, sleeping in barns on the way.'

What kind of work did you do on the farms?

'Not much, we had a guard, but we were mostly just passing time. We did as little as we could get away with! The last place I worked at was a cheese factory which we helped to build. I flew home when the war ended after V.E. day, then we were de-loused, bathed and supplied with clothes, then discharged.'

Have you visited the places where you were prisoner?

'No, I couldn't go there again. I

went on a rehabilitation course at Ilkley in Yorkshire when I got home. It's hard to settle down after being away so long, but I got a job with the Ministry of Pensions at Norcross in Blackpool for two years. When my brother came home from the army we took over mi dad's business of property repairing and maintenance. We were also into building. I retired on pension in 1979.'

Tell me what you did for entertainment when you were young?

'Well, we made our own fun. We went down Whalley in the summer. We used to play marbles and cigarette cards, buck and stick and hoopla. My father used to take mortar on a horse and cart to the builders, he supplied mortar for the builders in Fielding Lane and also in Hawthorn Avenue, when the houses were going up. We've allus worked hard though and taken an interest in everything we could.'

Tom Duckett

'I am the only Honorary Member of the Master Builders Federation in the country. It was an honour bestowed on me for the times I was president of the Federation.

My father, Ernest Duckett, always traded as Ernest Smith, but when my brother and I took over, we changed to our own name of Duckett. Where Bob Ireland's clogger's shop was at the end of Catlow Hall Street, used to be the harness room for the horses that pulled our waggonettes. My step-grandfather, Ernest Smith, was under contract to run waggonettes from the Golden Cross in Oswaldtwistle to Accrington on market days. The fare was just one old penny. Arthur Redford (I can see him now) was in his riding breeches with his leggings all polished up. When the waggonettes came back the first job was to 'root'

The Duckett brothers of Oswaldtwistle (Tom on the right, Francis on the left)

under the seats to see if anyone had dropped anything. Sometimes we'd find a half-penny; those were the days!

That land where the Pentecostal Chapel now stands used to be a big field just railed off, that's where my dad used to graze his horses in the summer. The most he ever had on were thirteen. They went to Belgium especially, to bring back two lovely Belgian horses. These horses were black all over and they stood sixteen hands. They were brought especially, to draw the hearse at a funeral and they wore

black plumes on their heads. They used to polish the hooves of these horses until they were like mirrors and they were shod at Bent Street farriers. I'm referring now to a horse my father had, which incidentally, dropped dead in front of the Palladium cinema. He was coming up from the gas works, pulling a cart with a load of ashes on when this happened. My father used these ashes to make mortar.

When I started work at fourteen, my father was friendly with a farmer called Charnley; a Town Bent farmer, so he found me a job as a farm labourer. This didn't do for me as I was getting up at five a.m., going to pick the dog up and bringing the cows in. I milked thirteen cows and when the other farm labourers were having a rest, I was put in the sand delph he owned, digging sand. I decided I wasn't going on with this job, so I started to work with mi father. (This is where we get back to the ashes). There were six or seven cotton mills around here and they emptied their fireboxes outside in a heap and I went round to collect them. Then I went to the office where I was given a 'chit' and at the weekend I used to get sixpence (2½p) a load; that money was a little extra fer miself. Anyhow, I fell out with mi father who told me to 'clear-off' and find meself another job, so I got a job with a builder and 'served mi time' which is how I got into the building trade.

I'll tell you about Town Bent pit if you're interested.'

Yes, please do.

'Well, Aspinalls here, the toffee shop, I used to 'mate' with Jim, the youngest lad. Every dinner-time he had to come home from school and three of his brothers worked at Town Bent pit. The mother had three dinners in basins, tied up in red hankerchiefs. We took these to the pit and put them, to keep warm, in the oven provided. When my dad's work was slack he used to buy bags of coal from there and go round selling it.'

Can you tell me some of the history of Oswaldtwistle?

'Well, Jackhouse is one of the Elizabethan buildings and during the war with Cromwell the residents of Jackhouse were evicted to make way for the Cromwells' sister. Cromwell came north to take Preston and his armies were kept at Longridge, which is how Longridge got it's name.

Apparently, when Cromwell was deploying his men he said, 'We'll put them on that long ridge', and so the name stuck! According to hearsay, the rightful owners took ninety years to regain possession of Jackhouse. I went up to paint a picture of the house when one half of it had collapsed. The owner invited me in and he showed me the great hall. Up high in the wall was a hole with light streaming through. Apparently cock fights were held there and they started when the sun shone through this hole into the centre of the room. We went up a stone spiral staircase and about half way up there was a six foot square flag about six inches thick. It seems that the food and grain were stored up there so that if the inhabitants were attacked by brigands, the family went upstairs and the man of the house could defend it from there.

What kind of winters did you have?

'When the weather was really bad some of our men were laid-off but then we got a telephone call from the Town Hall asking for a loan of our men and the wagons to help clear the centre of Accrington. I used to look through the window on a really bad morning with deep snow and wonder what work I could find for the men. There wer no work on the buildings and no dole, so the work for the council was a Godsend.'

You always had a good reputation, though.

'Well, we tried to be honest, and to do a good job. Mi brother was a prisoner of war for five years and I was in the army fer seven years. I went down on the *Lancastria* when it was bombed and I was one of the first off too, because I was blown off—I'd no option!'

Frank and Tom are still familiar figures in Oswaldtwistle to many people who know and respect them and they've both led very interesting lives.

‖‖‖‖‖‖‖‖‖‖‖‖‖‖‖‖‖‖‖‖‖‖‖‖‖‖‖‖‖‖‖‖‖

Harry Godbold
Miller Close, Oswaldtwistle

‖‖

'I was born and bred at 310 Union Road, Oswaldtwistle. It's a confectioner's neaw; then we went fro theear to Broadfield, 34 Broadfield. I went to school with the Rev. James Butterworth of Club Land. I went to school at two and a half in a tartan frock. I'd two—a red un and a green un. Rev. James Butterworth wore a velvet suit wi a yellow shirt an' a big pearl button. I went to Mount Pleasant School. I was one o' the boys out of eight local lads. When I were abeawt nine year owd I wer working fer Charlie Parr, goin' wi th' milk. I wer half time, four bob a week (20p), 5.30 a.m. 'til 9.30 a.m. then 4.30 p.m. 'til 8.30 p.m.; then I'd to av mi supper. I left theear an' I went in th' spinning room. I didn't like the spinning room at Stonebridge. Briggs wer the manager an' he lived at Broadfield house. I set off to go to th' spinning room one morning wi a potato pie in a dish, an' I getten work at Rushton [Rishton] pit. We 'ad a toffee shop at Broadfield. I geet two and ninepence eawt o' th' tin to pay Wright, School Board (truancy officer) fer mi papers to leave school.

I started at Rushton pit on mi thirteenth birthday, I stopped theear abeawt three years. I 'ad to leave because I split fireman's 'ead open wi mi lamp. I'd been crushed at pit, I'd three ribs broke, so they fun mi a leet job. I wer cleynin' windas deawn a pit—neaw then, heaw do you like thad? I wer at front o' th' engine eawse at bottom o' th' pit shaft. There were 144 windas at front o th' engine eawse, thad wer mi job all day, though.

I cut 'is 'ead oppen wi mi lamp, he'd to ev seven stitches, so I ed to leave. I've worked at a few pits: Huncoat, Dicky Brig, if ther wer any roof falls I'd to shift 'em. In th' 1921 coal strike, school board came but I told im to clear off. Then I went out croppin' – getting coil off th' top and selling id. At 1926 coil strike I kept Harlington bakery goin' wi coil fro up Hambledon, comin' deawn thad rooad reight facin' Griffin Pub. I geet wed i nineteen eighteen. Thad wer mi fost wife—who [she] died in 1941. I'd a lass at Foxhill.

I've done aw sooarts, I've done a days work bi ten o'clock at mornin': at Blythes I've filled twenty ton wi the bloody shuffle [shovel] then I've gone an done a full day by coiling [delivering coal].

I ad a horse and lorry, then I geet a motor lorry. I ad thad little farm at Broadfield wheear Tricketts is now. [Ice Cream people]. I went fra theear to th' Cobs at Cocker Brook when Jack o' Peas com to th' Rhoden. He wer at top farm and ad to stop avin' cattle on because o' pollution in th' reservoir. Tomlinson (Jack o' Peas) wed a lass cawed Moore, her brother wer a wrostler [wrestler]. He lived at number 6 Broadfield. He went from theear to Bowton [Bolton] where he bowt a wholesale greengrocers' business. Our Harry [his son] ad bi three year owd when I wed ar [her], mi second un—who were mi step sister, no relation, only mi mother married er father and I married er. During Second War I wer still baggin' coil, but I geet a bigger wagin an' wer doin' journey work.

I went to Hereford wi a buildin' firm. I carted mortar, on nights—thi were a firm cawed 'Garden of England'. When thi'd finished at Accrington wi went up whad thi

caw th' shoot at Haslingden, thi built some eawses theear. I carted motar from th' destructors to th' Willows Lane estate, and bagged coil i th' daytime. I've a jar o' thyme in th' cupboard yet. I puts id i' broth. Mi second wife, Maggie, I ed er nine year. I've never 'ad a silver weddin' and I've bin wed abeawt seventy year. After Maggie died I married another woman fro up Dill Hall. This woman, up Dill Hall, her dawter [daughter] wer one o th' usherettes wer I showed pictures an I ed awe th' usherettes squared [an under-standing]. Thi covered fer mi while I went to th' Printers Arms. I ed em trained to stop an heawr longer, while I went an ed a pint er two.

I used to go to th' slaughter eawse to buy mi meyt, then I used to sell id. When I left shouwin' pictures, I went to Stantons on th' pop job [selling minerals]. Place wert Black Dog, id wer a foundry afore id went on John Street. Stanton wer a trade name. I've ad third wife eighteen year, she wer

Harry Godbold, who has lived in Oswaldtwistle for 92 years

seventy three when she died. I bin married to Frances [fourth wife] sixteen year.

I used to go up Cocker Lumb, as a lad, pickin' mushrooms. There's no 312 Union Road, id wer put to 314, id wer a bit of a greengrocers. Thad's wer' Wood's Tinner shop started, then id went, just deawn Stonebridge Loine. Theear it's Gem Press neaw. Woods went theear, and then thi went in Victoria Street. I've ed a pass [free] an' I'm nod renewing id [for bus pass]. It costs £60 to renew thad fer me, an I goo eawt o th' eawse, on'y wi mi granchilden, thi tek mi in th' car, so why let the state pay £60 fer something I'm not going to use. I can't walk so far, so she 'as a wheelchair in th' back an' wheels mi reawnd th' supermarket. I geet measured fer a new suit fer mi grandawter geddin' wed. I wer measured 'ere in th' cheear [chair].

Derek Wynne cums ere every Wednesday to shave mi. I've ad some 'appy heawrs wi Derek—his father used to shave us in the air raid shelters in th' war. I sold mi coil business when I went in th' army an fost job I did i th' army wer gooin' reawnd wi bloody coil! I went to sign on an' thi sent mi to a bloody coil merchant! Thad wer in Coventry. I went fer 'oliday to a sister in law o'mine, I flit 'em theear. Well, I stopped in Coventry an' I geet wark, I worked at Standard [Motors], our John [his son] wer at Coventry.

I'm a life member at James Street Working Mens Club. It used to bi Pentecostal Mission, but thi cawed it 'Tin Hut'. James St. Club opened in two eawses in Albert Street, then thi come to James Street, and thad club as is theear today's built reawnd thad mission. Id oppened in 1912.

Bob Campbell and his father used to go to Fleetwood to buy fish. Thi used to stand near th' Central Club in Bridge Street, Accrington, to sell fish fra th' cart, to let coilliers av cheaper fish.

Then th' owd feller deed and Bob took thad shop. Id wer Gowards butchers when I lived theear.

There's still one or two characters in Ossie—thers Jack Flynn, lives in th' top eawse to th' Black Dog. He wer carding master at Vine [spinning] he wer robbed last week, while th' bin chaps wer at back dooar. Thi took over £300, he allus carried a lot o' money did Jack, cos he wer a bookie's runner, an he used to bet a lot hissel. He went livin' wi 'is dawter at Accrington.

I ed mi mother livin' wi mi, a took er all o'er when I wer working fer this building firm i Hereford. Sand wer sold bi th' yard theear, nod bi th' ton, an I bowt sand cheaper ner any man ever done. Thi used to measure yer wagin, id wer a chap an is two sons an th' mother; hi ed a bungalow and seven o' eight acre o' land. Aw this sand ad to bi getten wi, like a pick, id wer like gravel, sand, three and six a yard. I sez [this is when this thick eid gets gooin] 'heaw much is 1,000 yard? Thats this thick stuff id wer two and nine a yard. He sez: 'How much do you propose to pay for 1,000 yards?'

I sez: 'Ere you are, I'll fasten id wi £20 [deposit] and I'll pay every load now till I don't want no more then I'll wear thad twenty pound.'

Thad's eaw I beawt 1,000 yards o' sand.

I went to Rev. James Butterworth's funeral at Top Chapel—thi fetched im fra London, an all.

I put two lads to trade, one of em's a boss mechanic at Leavers today. Thad's mi coat of arms on th' wall, mi family tree, mi grandawter ged id fer mi. There's no so many people es ther own coat of arms in Ossie.

School Story

There wer a reindeer drawn on th' booard and th' teycher [teacher] wer askin' whad thad wer. Nobody knew whad id wer so teycher sez:

'Cum on Henry you'er a clever boy, you know whad id is don't you?

I sez: 'no teycher.'

She sez: 'Come on, whad does your father call your mother every Sunday morning?'

Harry is now over 90 years old. He had a party for his ninetieth birthday and still lives very comfortably with his fourth wife, Frances, who looks after him very well.

IIIIIIIIIIIIIIIIIIIIIIIIIIIIIIIIIIIIIIIIIIIIIIIIIIIIIII

Bill Salmon

ex-coalman from Oswaldtwistle

IIIIIIIIIIIIIIIIIIIIIIIIIIIIIIIIIIIIIIIIIIIIIIIIIIIIIIIIIIIIIIIIIIIIIIIIIIIIIIIIIIIIIIIIIIIIIIIIIIIIIIIIIIIIIIIIIIII

'I was born and bred in 6 Worsley Street and I went to St. Paul's School. Tom Heys was headmaster there then, a nice fellow wer Tom. I didn't do a lot of schooling because I wer never in the best of

Bill Salmon delivering coal to Mrs Eastwood in Oswaldtwistle

health. Kept gooing deawn to th' local doctor, Harry Fox, at the corner o' Frederick Street. He says to mi mother: 'When this lad starts work get im a job eawtside, because he'll not bi fit to work inside.' Sooa I started tekkin th' milk eawt fer Dick Ward. He had Higher Duckworth Hall Farm then, so I used to gooa wi th' milk at morning and then go t' school at th' afternoon, half-time. I left school at thirteen, when I went living on th' farm. It were too far to walk up at 5 o'clock at morning, so I had to live in. I were theear, well, as a matter of fact, I got married fra th' farm. I got married to a young woman called Ada Whittle who lived at Duck'orth Hall.

I started mi married life at bottom o' Duckworth Hill; there's three houses there locally known as 'Barker Nook', but actually it were New Lane.

It was 1937 when I left th' farm and I went working fer Jack Metcalfe on th' coal wagon. I moved into 41 Trinity Street then, and of course garage was up th' Nook then, and I used to do a lot o' removals. At that time, you know, people were leaving this district and gooin deawn to Coventry and Derby and them places an I reely enjoyed id, aye, I reely enjoyed id! Then war started, and I wer eawt wi beds fer evacuees. Jim (whad th' hell were he cawed; he lived in Worsley Street) He were on o' th' sweeper ups at Ozzy Teawn Hall. I've fergetten 'is last name. He used to go eawt wi mi after tay wi these beds wi th' flittin' van. We picked em up at th' Teawn Hall. They give us a list where we'd to tek 'em.

There were a few evacuees in Ozzy. Aye, there were some up New Lane. They went all o'er th' show. I think some of 'em, thi med their life 'ere—one or two on 'em, and some of 'ems bin back since, you know, to see the peopleas looked after 'em. Id were like owt else. We'd to do some fire watchin', so Metcalfe and me, we'd to join th' Fire Brigade. We used to go deawn theear, an' sleep theear two neets a week. If th' siren went in th' daytime when we were anywheer about, we used to dash in. At night I used to tek th' wagon deawn and I used to put a pump on it and ladders on. The Fire Station wer at th' bottom o' Tinker Brew. Prior to that, id wer a wheelright's shop. They used to mek carts and I forget name o' them as ed it an all neaw. Whcre t' Fire Station is now, it wer a big stone building. I think some of id ed bin part of a mill, because thi ed a cellar; id belonged to Ozzy Ceawncil, like. They used to tek coil theear, steam coil to run th' boilers, to keep id aired, you know. When they [the wheelrights] gave it up, they moved th' Fire Station from th' Teawn Hall to theear. Whatsaname, wer th' Fire Officer, Superintendent Pilling, Roland Pilling. He used to drive th' ambulance an' all, when th' bombers wer o'er.

There wer three bombs dropped in Ozzy. In John Street, there wer one dropped reight aside o' th' joiners shop (Walsh's), and then there wer one dropped aside New Inn in a (Whad street's thad?) I've fergetten th' name o' bloody street neaw. Anyway there wer one dropped theear, an' one wer dropped in Havelock Street and th' third one wer dropped in er . . . (what the hell's it cawed?), side o' th' New Inn . . .

Thomas Street!

Oh, they med a reight bloody mess. We went up, aye, we went up an' there were bloody slutch [mud] all o'er. There wer nobody reely hurt, but it did a lot o' damage and 'ow you've 'eard o'er people saying o' th' bombs lifti' big pieces o' masonry? Well, you know them kerbstones what they 'ad on th' flags; they'd be abeawt four er five inches thick and 'appen a yard long? id 'ed lifted one o' them on the slates (roof) in Havelock Street; aye, onto number forty-one.

A fellow cawed Fred Ratcliffe lived theear, an' he wer in th' Fire Service, an' he says to Pilling, he says like:

'Is it possible fer me to goo hoam, super?'

He says: 'What fer, Fred?'

He says: 'Well, they've dropped a bloody bomb at t' side o' mi heawse.'

He says: (An' this is the point abeawt it) 'I've getten a £5 nooat upstairs in th' drawer.'

He wer only bothered abeawt bloody £5 nooat. Anyway he went and 'is £5 nooat wer still theear, but they'd med a mess of 'is heawse.

Then later on, you know wi the war there wer doodlebugs [V Bombs]. There wer one came over us an' it dropped on Cocker Brook. I've fergotten name o' that damn farm, neaw! Peter Grimshaw wer theear at the time. As a matter o' fact, I 'eard it, you know, gooing up our street, we heeard it gooah, and there wer a bloody bang, but id ed dropped in a field an' didn't do much damage to th' farm. We went up theear, weh [well] you couldn't star [stir] fur bloody slutch and muck. It sent some slutch up and I think t' others as wer dropped wer Ribchester way. I think I recollect thad. Them two heawses at Altham, wer don wi th' bombs. Thad wer another comedy at th' Fire Station. There wer two heawses hit; there's a space theear yet. Whatsaname wer on thad neet, Jimmy Abbot. It warned owr neet on and Tommy says:

'If owt goes wrong, ring, Jimmy.'

Bang.

Abbot picks up the 'phone and Tommy says:

'What's to do, Jimmy?'

He says: 'They're eear!' and he banged th' bloody 'phone deawn.

He says to us th' day after— anybody could 'ave been 'ere, he just said, 'hey're eear!' He wer a comic, wer Jimmy, he wer a grand lad though, he lived up Duke Street, 'e wer alreight.

Then, there wer them 'as dropped in Blackburn, they went o'er th' Fire Station; oh aye, it wer a reet moonlit neet. We wer talkin' in t' garage. I ad mi wagon, as I used to drive 'cause they'd two wagons. Well. this bloody thing comes o'er, we heeard it and we all dropped o' th' flooar, th' lot on us, and id went past and we heeard th' bang. It dropped in Penny Street at Blackburn. But they didn't send us theear, Blackburn lads went.'

Did you go to Sunday School?

'No, I didn't go th' Sunday School. You see, wi working at th' farm, id wer too far to come deawn. I never come hooam after I wer thirteen, I slept at th' farm. I worked from 5 o'clock in th' morning 'til 5 o'clock at neet; sometimes 6 o'clock at neet!

I don't believe Duckworth Hall Pub was the Hall itself, because ther wer a farm next dooar; thad ad some o' them medivil [medieval] windas in, so id could've bin th' Hall, but I don't know any history abeawt thad. I know one of Hindles 'as 'ad a farm up th'Nook, one o' th' lads, he went livin' theear.

I started wi Metcalfe on th' coil wagon in 1937 an' id built up a lot. He 'ad a lot o' customers i' Accrington and when th' war came on, of cooarse, you'd to register wi a coil merchant, an' a lot o' customers registered their relations, so it kind of built up.

I used to work all Accrington. I'd a full week's wark in Accrington. We got our coil fra' Leyland Street Sidings—it allus came by rail; it wer all Yorkshire coil, an' some used to come from Burnley, from Towneley Pit. It wer pretty good coil, wer thad, but majority on id wer Yorkshire. Then we used to do th' flittings [removals] in between. Tha knows he'd a' come [Metcalfe] and he'd say: 'Tha's a flittin' this afternoon, ged on wi thi wark this morning,' and I'd to bloody catch up after wad I 'adn't done! I took over the business in 1961 because he went livin' at Blackpool. I flit 'im to Blackpool.

He worked at Town Bent Pit, did Jack Metcalfe, and 'e used to tek coil eawt. Town Bent coil wer mostly fer Ozzy Co-op customers. He 'ad a whatsaname then, a horse and cart. After th' war (That wer th' Fost World War) he started on his own. They [Town Bent Pit] said they could 'ave their own horses and carts and buy their coil off th' pit. That's eaw he started 'is coil round on his own. The he geet fairly big so he geet a little motor. Rex, my son, now runs the business, but it's not as big as it wer. I used to enjoy id. I'd allus a good relationship wi mi customers. I know there wer one up Rawson Avenue; I'd eight er nine customers in Rawson Avenue. Well, in winter time it used to be bloody awful gedding up them backs. I used to leave th' wagon at top and walk deawn and empty th' bloody bins—they wer full of ashes, otherwise you couldn't stop. One woman says: 'Tha'll cop id,'

I says: 'Bugger 'em,' I says: 'It'll save 'em emptying 'em.'

They were good customers were them. I went one morning and who [she] were playing hell o'er th' last lot o' coil. Who says: 'What sooart of sh** 'es ta fetched mi?'

I says: 'It's good is this, Mrs Wells.'

Who went on playing bloody hell you know, and I just stood theear. Who says: 'It no use talking to thi, is id?'

I says: 'Ev you finished neaw?'
Who says: 'Aye.'
I says: 'Well God bless you.' I says: 'Put th' kettle on, I won't be long afore I'm here.'

I geet on like heawse on fire wi the customers, no trouble at all, but a lot o' them owd customers has gone you know. There's only two coal merchants now. There used to be sixty odd coil chaps i' Accrington and Ozzy. They're only

little rounds, you know.

Two of mi relations, (twins) they used to call 'em 'Cuckoo Brothers'. Ben and Joe Woodhead. They were 'ard as nails. They called 'em th' cuckoo brothers' because they used to go a poaching. Poaching wer rife in them days. If one 'ad getten a rabbit, or whatever he'd getten, he'd pud 'is 'ands to 'is meawth and he'd sheawt: 'Cuckoo!' and you could 'ear id fer miles.

And thi, whatsaname, they worked at Town Bent Pit and they used to go round working on th' farms, and I know mi grandad were warking on th' farm at Cooach 'an 'osses, and thi wer 'aving a bet one day and he [Woodhead, I presume] jumped off slates wi umbrella fer a parachute. Silly bugger broke 'is leg and that was all fer a beer tha knows, a couple o' pints a beer and they'd damn near kill thersell. Then one day he went deawn to th' barbers at side o' th' library. When barber shaved 'im he says: 'By gum, Ben, tha's a strong beard.'

He says: 'Aye, dosta know, bi half past four this afternoon, it'll have grown ageean.'

He says: 'Well if it does, I'll shave tha fer nowt.'

Anyway he goes up to his twin brother and he says: 'Est ta 'ed a shave today?'

'Naw,' he says.
'Well go deawn to th' barbers at half past four.'

So he goes deawn, goes walking in, and th' barber looks at 'im. He says: 'By gum, Ben, tha's reight— ged in th' chair and I'll shave thi fer nowt.'

That's how they were, you couldn't tell one fra t'other. In the old book of Oswaldtwistle, their names are in. Aye I allus says mi ancestors are in th' Ozzy book. They wer two characters, th' wer thad.'

Unfortunately, both his son Rex, and his wife, Ada have died since this

interview, but Bill still manages to keep cheerful and maintain his marvellous sense of humour. He is now remarried and lives in Blackburn.

August 1989—Shortly after this interview, Bill himself was taken ill and didn't recover; but I'm glad that I was able to speak to him and record something of his life.

‖‖

Joe Holmes

retired miner from Oswaldtwistle

‖‖

Where were you born and bred then, Joe?

'Up Belthorn in 1908; mi father wer killed in the First World War. We've lived in Church, Green Haworth, then eventually in Accrington. I went to St. James's School, which I left at fourteen. I started work in 1922 and wer offered a job at Luptons at 10/3d a week [approximately 51p]. But I found out I wer able to earn 17/4d [approximately 87p] at the pit, so that's where I went. I got a job at Whinney Hill Pit quite by accident. The lad that was with me, worked at Luptons and in the process of seeing the pit manager (who didn't really want any lads) discovered that the lad with me, called Cowgill, was the son of a former employee, so we got the job and I started at Whinney Hill Pit. I went to work on the Tuesday following the Friday when I'd left school.

The first day underground, we were given an oil lamp with one eighth of a candle power light. We got on a wooden sledge and wer taken about two miles underground, under Great Harwood football ground, so I wer told. Inside, after half an hour, someone came and took mi lamp away fer a collier who wer getting coal when his lamp went out. I wer left in total darkness; stripped to a pair of shorts and bare feet. I had to help push the wagons of coal up a brow as they came from the coal face. The first day I wer told to roll up mi shirt and stuff it into mi cap as I had to put mi head to the tub to push it along. Later I got a bag full of cork dust from the greengrocer, put it into a bag and sewed it up; that wer the 'Thrutcher'. I wer terrified when I wer left alone in the dark, but I had to stick it out—it wer an adventure!

I've trained lads since as I became an official of the N.C.B. A Mr Jeremiah, who wer on Clayton-le-Moors council, was mi training officer. I called mi group of trainees together and told them of mi experiences with a warning that if they ignored the rules they would be 'sacked' on the spot, with no appeal. I'd been through it, and if I could help it no-one else would have it as hard. I got sacked at Whinney Hill after twelve months. I'd advanced from 'pushing up'—to 'drawing' and obviously wasn't speedy enough fer the collier I worked for. He used to put a hot lamp on mi naked buttock which caused me to bang mi back on the roof. I got boils on mi back, which were knocked off with the roof and thi wer very sore. I had an iron bar in the tub and when I reached a place where I could stand up I

'lashed out' at this man. (The colliers had all the rights.) I wer fined 5/- [25p] and then 'sacked'. I went in the 'ring frame' department at Howard and Bulloughs fer two weeks. I wer told to put a heavy box on a truck and push it across the floor with the nuts and bolts in; they wouldn't let me carry them! I then went to work at Huncoat Pit.

When I turned up on Monday morning I'd to start on the pit top. I'd got a reputation fer striking a collier, which wer a serious offence, so it wer the pit top 'er nothing! I wer tipping and grading coal—a hell of a dusty job! Thi call that place: 'The Black Hole of Calcutta!' We opened the windows to let the dust blow out and the women of Huncoat complained about dust on ther washing. Ther wer coke ovens at Huncoat and the hot coke wer raked out manually with a long handled rake. In summer these men started work at 4 a.m. because of the heat from the ovens. Then one day along came the manager to tell us that they wanted lads underground. I'd got used to the job on the surface so I refused to move, so again I'd to choose; either go underground 'er finish! Then I wer working underground fer the next twenty-five years. I've done every job underground except being an official! I've been a 'drawer', which means taking coal from the face to the haulage. We then brought back the empty tub and any supports [pit props] the miner needed. The collier wer on 'piece work' so we had to keep up with him. The 'drawers' asked fer more wage when the miners wer mechanised and eventually we got ten bob [50p] a day, which wer very good in them days. We worked an eight hour shift up to 1926, there was a slogan:

'Eight hours work and eight hours pay,

Eight hours sleep and eight bob a day!'

As we got older we wer given the job of laying the tracks on which the haulage ran and changing supports where the roof had crushed them. We did any job away from the coal face. We also had to make the roadway fer the tubs. The machines wer installed after the strike in 1926 and improved things a lot. These machines wer introduced in the parts of the country where the coal seams were thickest. Hargreaves' Colliery at Clayton-le-Moors wer being put out of business. Also the coke works wer being built. No miners wer willing to accept machinery—it was the fear of being put out of work which wer the main reason. The men were bullied into acceptance of the machines. Jobs wer hard to get so we had to 'bow the knee' to machinery and the losses.

I did a period of coal cutting; ther wer three men on a machine; driver, back man and a man to look after the cables. These cables wer as thick as a man's arm and thi took a lot of handling. The cable had to pass under a low roof and had a tendency to spring back and turn a man over. Mining wer a very skilled job, although people didn't realise this then. Miners had to get coal fer many years using only lamps which gave very inadequate light and this caused eye trouble. When electric lighting wer introduced, of course, there wer a big improvement and the miners' sight wer saved.

Town Bent Pit wer closed down after the roadways caved in. The miners got work at Huncoat and Scaitcliffe Pits. Hargreaves' Colliery started their own domestic fuel supply. When I got married the first time and changed mi address I was told that either I bought mi coal at Hargreaves' Colliery or I was finished. As a newly married man I got a penny a bag discount. There was a John Hargreaves & Co. at Burnley, George Hargreaves at Accrington and when Altham

Coke Works wer established, they merged together to guarantee supplies to the coke works. The major shareholders were the 'McAlpines'. Hargreaves' wer members of a Bolton family.

Doctor Barlow's house wer destroyed in the Second World War. The bombers wer after the coke works which then had to be shielded so the glare couldn't be seen from above. 'Dicky Brigg' Pit wer on the canal bank and was so named because the bridge wer very fragile; the correct name was Moorfield Colliery. When the Second World War started I wer asked to work afternoons fer two weeks but did seven years instead. I asked fer a change and wer put on nights; the money wer better and I got so used to working nights that I didn't want to come off.

In the meantime, a John Riley [one time Mayor of Accrington] wer working at Scaitcliffe Pit. He came on the day shift as a collier and I took over his place 'ripping' on the night shift. 'Ripping' consisted of drilling the roof then having it blown down and packed at either side to make roadways. The roadways wer eight feet wide and six feet high and wider on the haulage way. Ther wer also a ventilation factor. From Hoddlesden to Belthorn, the underground is riddled with mines, even up to Baxenden. In the olden days, miners used to break into the hillside, get out as much coal as they could, then break in somewhere else. Long ago farmers may have found this black shiny stuff which had been washed out by the rain. Then they found that it would burn and so the mining industry started.

When the 1926 coal strike wer on, people went up Moleside and Hambledon to the abandoned open cast mines, looking fer coal, but it wer very soft coal! People wer unaware of the dangers involved in mining the coal without disturbing the roof. This country has wasted

its most precious asset by burning raw coal on open fires. Ther are two thousand by-products fer tar alone, which is a by-product of coal. As I said, though, I followed John Riley as a 'ripper' and I also followed him as secretary of the Accrington Branch of the N.M.U. He became part of the Ministry of Fuel and Power, which was set up in wartime. We classed ourselves as an intelligent branch of the miners' union. This area had six days' pay fer five days' work as far back as I can remember. Hargreaves' Collieries weren't all that bad though. They agreed that afternoon and night shift wer unpleasant and agreed to pay miners fer six days insted of five. When war started they tried to make the miners work a seven-day week, but after a lot of debate we compromised on a six-day week fer the day shift. We had a long battle with the Ministry of Fuel and Power before they accepted it, though. However, thi got ther own back when Calder Pit went on strike over some local dispute. It wer, of course, illegal to strike in wartime, so the branch wer taken to court and fined £300 We didn't have 300 pennies to our name, let alone £300, so we had to devise ways and means of paying the fine. That was when the miners' 'pool' started.

The miners are a great set o' mates, but if you cross them, they'll fight like mad. Miners work hard; play hard; swear hard; everything they do is hard; so if thi get ther 'knife' into you it goes in hard! I signed an agreement at Huncoat fer one shilling below what the rippers wanted and the first comment I wer greeted with when I came into the office was: 'Throw 'im down t'bloody shaft!' Thi didn't know another increase wer in the pipeline—but I did. Of course, when thi became aware that thi would gain—eventually—nothing wer too good fer me! The mines became nationalised in 1947 and I'd been invited to apply to be

Labour Officer fer this area. We wanted representatives fer our smaller area which couldn't compete with the five- and six-foot coal seams of Manchester and Wigan. My responsibility was fer the wages and working conditions of the men. I made it a policy to go down every pit fer which I wer responsible, to see fer miself what the conditions wer like. The only time I worried wer when I wasn't in trouble; that wer when I wondered who wer hatching plots. At that time nationalisation wer needed as everything had been run down during the war. No colliery in the country could afford to re-equip. The government of the day had to finance the most proficient pits, so we, as the poor relation, had to struggle fer what we could get. However, we made progress indeed; Burnley area wer the first pit in the North West to make a profit. Burnley had the thinnest coal seams and the smallest work force in the country. Rossendale Valley had a few pits—Holme Meadow; Stonebridge; one at the top of the hill between Bacup and Todmorden. At one time ther wer twenty-three pits in this area. Burnley took over the pit at Padiham which had a nine-foot seam. There wer also a 'short life' drift at Higham, along with others in the area. That wer first-class house coal! The colliery at Cliviger had, at one time, in the 1930s, supplied coal to Buckingham Palace. That wer written in the records at Cliviger when the pits were nationalised. The firemen at that time, wer paid 1/- [5p] per shift and lads of eight years old wer paid a penny a day fer a twelve hour shift. These boys sat there all day opening the doors, by pulling a string, to let the tubs of coal come through. At the time when ponies wer used down the pits, they wer only brought to the surface fer one week in the year. That wer the only time thi saw daylight. and breathed fresh air. They wer the small Shetland ponies. Cruel as this may seem, they were the best cared-for creatures that went underground. Ther stables at the shaft wer clean and warm and the animals wer well fed. The ponies wer used to haul the heavy wagons to the shaft bottom where they wer then hauled to the surface. When a man couldn't do this the pony did, so thi wer a valuable asset to the mine owners.

When the colliers wer coming out of Whinney Hill, before ther wer Pit Head baths, a lady from Preston wer once visiting her sister in Dill Hall Lane. The miners wer walking down the lane when the visitor saw them. 'Oh,' she said to her sister: 'Haven't you got a lot of chimney sweeps here?'

Everything that came to be used in the pit wer called a 'strong-arm patent' by the miners, because all the equipment wer very heavy. I wer Industrial Officer fer the Burnley miners, which, included Altham Coke Works. I'd to learn all about this. I knew 'sweet fanny adams' about carbonisation etc., so I'd to learn! I'd helped to produce the raw material, coal, but then I'd to learn about processing it through the plant so as to be in a position of knowledge when I had to negotiate wages and conditions.

Coke work wer a seven-day week, 365 days a year job. The men had ther days off, so thi accepted the weekend work. On one occasion ther wer a dispute at Altham Coke Works. I brought the 'Director' from Manchester and we had a discussion, but we had to adjourn every half an hour to turn the ventilator over.

The steel industry used most of the Altham coke—it had to be especially hard fer steel smelting. It wer also producing gas fer all the district. Towards the end of its life no-one wanted the coke, but there was a great demand for the gas. We had to continue producing coke we didn't want in order to provide the gas. So, although the coke was a financial loss, we provided the public with gas.

I enjoyed mi work; it wer like chasing a girl. The thrill isn't in the conquest; it's in the hunt! I could talk to any man about his job and could plan, mentally, how to go about it. When I wer a trade unionist, we used to have meetings with Colonel Bolton at Highbrake Hall. There wer always a drink and a cigar when we went in December, along with a Christmas present.

We used to drag the tin bath into the front room in front of the fire, and sometimes there wer four er five colliers in a family. The colliers who'd no sons would go to an orphanage and adopt a son to be his 'drawer'. They'd all bath in the same water in front of the fire. Wives thought nothing of washing the backs and fronts of their men if necessary. There wasn't much illness amongst the miners; the weaklings either got out or were 'kicked' out by the management! When the pits were mechanised, the management chose the most docile men to stay on; it wer survival of the fittest.

There are known quantities of coal from here to Preston; but it's 600 yards deep and it's full of sulphur, which is the worst thing that could happen. Before I finished I wer in charge of industrial relations in the whole of Lancashire. I had to take care of Manchester, North Wales as well as Burnley and eventually Cumberland. There's still a lot of coal underground the Manchester Ship Canal from Liverpool to Manchester. Someday this coal will be recovered if only for its by-products. We found fossils in the seams; fish bones, leaves etc. Mining's a fascinating industry apart from the hard work. There was an attempt to standardise the name of the same job done in different pits but it took a long time to get the different pits to agree to this. This helped us to agree on a wage structure throughout the industry though. When I wer working at Whinney Hill, the cages got stuck in the shaft and we had to go through the area of a previous explosion which happened in 1883. Nearly one hundred men wer killed in that explosion between Moorfield and Martholme Grange colliery. I probably owe mi life to a mouse, though. As I said, as a lad I had to sit by the doors ready to push the tubs up the hill. Once a mouse appeared so I got up to grab it just as the roof caved in where I'd been sitting. People who suffer from claustrophobia can't stand working in the mines; others can't be in total darkness so they don't stop; they 'pack-up' right away!

When I was in charge of the coke works, we wer attached to Yorkshire because Altham wer the only coke works in Lancashire. We had to go to Yorkshire which had six er seven coke works, whenever negotiations on wages were needed. I bumped into Arthur Scargill on one of these occasions. He always wanted to be on the front row shouting the odds. Joe Gormley and I used to have a pint in the Royal Oak in Manchester when I was in that area. We settled many an argument there between ourselves. Joe Gormley delayed his resignation fer twelve months to prevent Mick Magahi taking over the presidency in London. Joe Gormley wer a sensible, level-headed chap, very good at his job. When I retired I wer Deputy Director fer Industrial Relations; this covered all the North Western area, in 1969. I wer 'knocked down' a few times but I had to get up, shake mi head and carry-on from there. Two of the hardest things I had to do were:
1. Notify the family of anyone killed at the pit. The first one wer a man of 26 at Cliviger and I had to break the news to his wife. She had a young child and another due within a few months. I don't know

how I got through that, to tell her about it.

2. The time I had to tell mi sister-in-law that mi brother had been killed at Thornley Bank Pit. I remembered one widow I offered mi sympathy to, she said: 'Aye lad, don't feel sorry fer me, he wer never any bloody good!'

A miner calling to tell another widow that her husband had been killed said: 'I'm sorry Mrs Jones, can I have his clogs?'

What a wonderfully interesting person Joe Holmes was to talk to. Reliable,

hardworking, sensible and very fair. I can understand how he rose from an ordinary pit boy to his well-deserved position of Deputy Director of Industrial Relations when he reired. He is an example to us all!

‖‖

Jimmy Stephenson

past-owner of Ossie's famous 'Potato Pie Shop'

‖‖

'I was born at 17 White Ash Lane, Oswaldtwistle. I went to Immanuel School and Mr Whittle was headmaster there. Miss Connie Hindle was one of the teachers. Then I came down to Moorend School, which was newly built. I was amongst the first pupils at Moorend. We stayed there while we wer fourteen, then we left school.

I started work at Lang Bridges as an apprentice moulder. I stayed there until late 1946, then I went into the pie-shop at the corner of Cross Street. I didn't like moulding but going in this pie-shop was something that 'just happened'.

I lived in the White Bull prior to going into the pie-shop. I went into the 'Bull' in 1928, this was in New Lane opposite Immanuel Church. I was 11 when I went into the White Bull with my parents. There wer a load of characters that came into that pub. Beer was served in pint pots and quite a few of the customers had their own pint pots. They never changed a note in the tap room, they would sit in the tap

room, order a pint and come to th' bar to change it. That carried on until after th' war—they were scared o' somebody seeing thi' 'ad a note and tryin' to borrow off them, you see. Thi used to play at dominoes fer the honour an glory; thi weren't bothered over a sixpence er shilling, they were only interested in winning. One er two of 'em, when thi got beat, used to go 'ome an' sulk.

Then in 1947 we went to live in the cook-shop at the corner of Cross Street. It must be very famous because everyone talks about it yet after all these years. Ernie Riley 'ad it before; he took it just after the First World War and Tom Helm's parents 'ad it before them. It appears we've bin thought better of since we cum eawt (of the shop) ner what we were when we were in! After the Second World War everything was still rationed, but wi got allocations of course. It wer difficult but it weren't difficult selling. Everything you med just went you see, the main problem was when we cum off rationing.

There were seven mills shut up [closed] and there were two or three other cook-shops so I decided to shut up as well and just open weekends until things cum back to normal, which I did, fer a few years. Then things cum back to normal, we opened regular and wi did very well. I worked at Cockers during the week when the shop was shut and we just opened weekend. We med potato pies; steak pies; steak puddings etc. We started full time again in the shop about ten years ago [1976]. I did the baking and mi wife helped o' course.

I weren't a confectioner; that's a different set-up. It weren't a money spinner really, weren't shop, it weren't open long enough. You could mek a wage but it were only a dinner-time shop an' a supper-time shop. I had to cut one supper time out 'else I'd o' bin working eight days a week!

I think the new supermarket [Gateway] is a good thing fer Ossie, because ninety five percent of 'Ossies' went to Accrington fer their big buying-in [weekly shopping]. I think it's ideal. In days gone by people used to go to Blackpool, now they go to Winfields, Tommy Balls and Asda for a day out.

I went to Sunday School at Immanuel. I wouldn't say I wer carried away wi it. I think if we ed'nt bin med to go to th' Sunday School wi might a carried on going, but the majority of us were med to go to th' Sunday School and wi didn't like going so wi stopped away.

When wi were in th' White Bull, wi'd a Jack Hulme playin' the piano and wi had a good singin' room. There were some good singers used to ged up. I 'ad some 'appy times livin' at th' 'Bull', though God knows what their rent is neaw! Wi never 'ed any Sunday School picnics. I went on a young men's picnic once, but thad's better fergetten. Ther wer a beer shortage, you know. Non-drinkers said, 'We're only 'eving one er two then wer off.' (Blackpool was the venue.) This·wer abeawt 8 o'clock. So at 10 o'clock wi all cum eawt o' th' pub, except all th' teetotallers— thi never moved. Typical Sunday Schoo' stuff, an' I 'eard more nasty jokes on that trip than I ever 'eard in mi life!

Wi ed a lot a weddings to cater for when wi were in th' cook-shop; sum successful; sum not, sum divorced.

James St. Club used to be called 'The Tin Hut'. It had been a church and the club took id over. Tinker Brew used to bi th' best tradin' place in Ossie. It was very built-up in them days, they all 'ed big families. I've 'eard 'em seh that i Ash Street they used to drag all th' kids in anybody's 'eawse, thi didn't bother wer thi belonged; thi used to ged 'em ready fer Sunday morning then send 'em 'ooam. I allus lived up th' top end o' Ossie, I'm a top-ender, me, allus lived above th' lamp. Bear in mind there wer sum up theear never cum deawn Ossie at all, only to t' pictures. Thi 'ed Bob Clarke's shop up theear—id wer a good shop, you know, nod prices up and deawn like thi are neaw. You could ged anything you wanted up theear, then Bob's wife died.

Mr. Hesketh, the librarian, was very strict but he was very efficient. You daren't leave any finger marks on th' books and as fer kids running up and deawn like

thi do neaw, there'd a bin an execution!'

Jimmy and his wife are remembered for their delicious potato pie more than anything else. The shop they had has been pulled down now, but everyone who sees Jimmy reminds him of his work.

||||||||||||||||||||||||||||||||||||||||||||||||||||||||||

Harry Salt

ex-councillor, Church Urban District Council

||||||||||||||||||||||||||||||||||||||||||||||||||||||||||

Where were you born then, Harry?

'Canal Street, Church, and I went to Church Kirk School. I think I had one of the best teachers anyone could have had—Mrs Golden. I never knew that lady raise her hand to anyone and her knowledge of County Cricket was second to none! We had some really good teachers—Mrs Palmer; Miss Taylor; Miss Grimshaw etc.

Church Kirk was a poor locality but the people were honest. You could leave your door open anytime and they'd always help one another. From Church Kirk School I went to Rhyddings; I didn't get into further education. I then went

working at the print works down Foxhill Bank and I was called up into the Navy in 1914.'

I understand that your family originated as canal people?

'Yes, they came from the Kidderminster area. They'd always worked on the boats and used to bring salt from Northwich to William Blythes at Church. Grandma Salt used to go with the second boat when they took salt to Blythes chemical works and brought other goods back. They worked between Manchester and Liverpool. When they were building the aqueduct at the iron bridge, they brought bales and bales of cotton. The land was a swamp, the railway lines were built on trestles. (I think.)'

Where was that at, then?

'Hapton Valley. My grandparents then got a house near Blythes. Grandad worked at Blythes a while, then went back on the boats working on the Leeds and Liverpool canal. All his brothers were bargees as well.

Joseph was my grandad's name; he could neither read nor write but he knew what money was. In those days the boat men had to buy their own horses. They used ex-funeral horses; why, I don't know. Uncle Joe went with him, but he went further afield on the Manchester Ship Canal. Uncle Fred also went on the boats. He could neither read nor write but he was a character in his own right as well. He was a very heavy drinker and he came home one night and gave his wife a black eye. When he awoke the following morning he said: 'Who the hell's done that.'

'You did, last night,' she told him, and he never touched alcohol again 'till the day he died!

He was going abroad in 1939 and he went all over the world despite being unable to read and write.

Uncle George lived at New Brighton and he worked on the River Mersey. Uncle Jim worked on the River Weaver on the I.C.I. salt boats. Uncle Ted, at Northwich, also worked on the canal. My great aunt was a typical 'water gypsy'; all the jewellery she wore was solid gold; you couldn't cheat her, she was quite a character!

Old grandad told this story about his father: When he died he was given a boatman's funeral and they had to use a crane to lift him out of the boat. I believe he weighed twenty seven stones.

When uncle Bill started work, half-time, he went to work at the canal wharf at Church Commercial and he had the same wage as a man. He worked on the 'fly' boats, which meant changing the horses every so often. When they brought the sugar back to Blackburn, there was so much for Enfied at Clayton-le-Moors and so much for Burnley; then they went on to Skipton and Leeds. They re-loaded with cement or anything else that was going. On the Leeds and Liverpool Canal there are two tunnels and if the steamer didn't take the boat through, you had to 'leg it' on a plank. We got three shillings extra for negotiating the Gannow Tunnel at Burnley. The tunnel at Foulridge is not quite a mile long and we got five shillings for that. No matter the weather, rain; snow or frost, I never knew a boatman suffer from the common cold.'

Why was that?

'Well, being out in the fresh air, and good wholesome food—not the rubbish we have today. We'd eggs; bacon; cheese; meat etc. On the Leeds and Liverpool Canal at Bingley a man called Turner had a big orchard near the locks. We could get a bucket full of apples and a dozen eggs for a shilling [5p]. We went to Shipley; a load here, a load there, a twelve or fourteen hour day was common. The old horse used to plod along but we stopped to feed him of course. Woe betide any bargee who ill-treated his horse, he was sent to 'Coventry'! And I mean sent to Coventry!

When the canals were frozen over, then they used ice-breakers and they were very hard work. The horses had to pull hard to get the boats through and sometimes an explosive had to be used to clear the way. After the Leeds and Liverpool Canal Company, grandad went to work for Ben Walls at Skipton. He had brand new boats all called by a letter from the Greek alphabet. Grandad got a boat called The Omega which, in Greek, meant 'the end'. I was only four years old but I well remember being given a shilling for saying the word 'Omega'.'

Why was Church so well used as a loading point?

'Well, 95% of Howard and Bulloughs machinery was transported by canal and also Steiners Calico Printworks and Foxhill Bank Printworks used the canal transport. Steamers used to come up the canal; 130 tons of goods could be carried. I think that in the future someone will have to start thinking about re-using the canals; not only to protect the environment, but to make better use of fuel. I've seen wagons waiting for days to be unloaded at Liverpool when the goods could have been carried by boats. Blackburn was a busy centre. The boatmen used to leave the boat at Blackburn and catch the tram to Church where they would spend a night at home. They would come back with a huge basket full of food. There was never any stealing but I never knew grandma Salt to buy any coal. The coal which was left after being washed-off the boat was put in bags and it was my job, when we got to Church Wharf, to fetch this coal on a truck. Everybody was happy and they all worked together but they had their moments like us all.

Where the old Copy Clough sewage works used to be, lived a chap who was nicknamed 'Muck Bill'. He used to take all the sewage to the Flyde for fertilizer.

There was the 'Black Diamond' boating company at Blackburn; Crook and Thompson; Appleby's Grain Boats etc. Grandad went to work on the boats at Skipton but they're all closed down now. When grandad decided to leave the boats he got a job at Blythes Chemical Works at Church. During the war, uncle Bill left his boat on the canal at Liverpool and it was sunk during an air-raid. Of all the men I met on the canal, very few of them used obscene language. Also, Rector Stephens was a well-known character in this parish, (Church Kirk) a great bloke. If you got grandad Salt, Rector Stephens and Mrs Furness, who had a shop in Walmsley Street, on a Wednesday afternoon, having a drink of tea with a drop of whisky in, you wouldn't get served in the shop fer love ner money. They used to talk about old times—Kidderminster way. One child once came to grannie and said, 'They've just pulled somebody out of the canal at t' swing bridge.' Five minutes later owd Joe Martin came (the local bobby).

Our grannie was the local midwife and 'washer-out' at the mortuary. For that she got half a crown [25p]. There was a man who lived in Commercial Street who murdered his wife. Grandma Salt laid her out and stopped with the doctor at the mortuary until the pathologist came.

People had family squabbles and they drank, but there was little thieving. Farhomes, called locally 'Faroons', down Aspen Valley, was the home of a self-employed grave-digger and a linoleum fitter. I never knew them to work, but they always had change for a five pound note. Mr Taylor had a small-holding down near the little bridge. He had no gas; no electricity; no indoor toilet; got his water from a spring, then walked up that hill with a basket of eggs, two and three times a day. One Sunday morning they were all sat on the big stone by the canal. Rector Stephens was talking to them when Mr Taylor came up.

'Good morning, Mr Taylor,' said the rector.

Mr Taylor was stone deaf and he said, 'Eh, I can't hear you for the bells.'

He liked a pint of beer to which he added a piece of chopped camphor.'

What was that for?

'Well, I don't know really, but he lived to be over ninety. Old grandad lived to be eighty-seven, he only had one tooth missing! When he was eighty, he fell off a canal boat, had suffered a broken leg; arm and several ribs, also a fractured skull. The doctor at the hospital said he wouldn't live till morning, so I said I'd stop because he was unconcious. Twenty past five in the morning a voice called out, 'Where's mi breakfast?' He had his eightieth birthday in the hospital and recovered.'

What about any characters in Church?

'Well, we had a lot but I should think 'Owd Gough' who lived in Albert Street wer one of the best known. I never knew him miss a day's work. His knowledge of cricket wer second to none and he had a unique record. He'd been thrown off every ground in the Lancs league! His mate wer Jimmy Kenyon and they all used to meet in the Church Commercial to have a drink, call in at the 'Hare and Hounds' to have one there then go up to the cricket ground at West End. They used to 'feel' the

Chairman of Church Council 1971-72, Harry Salt, and his wife Elsie

wicket; Ted Hartley; Tommy Law; Walter Lomax; all the lads who played fer Church and Dick Duckworth.'

What about Harry Turner's chip shop?

'Oh, Harry Turner. Tha could get fish and chips there at half past one in a morning and they were the best fish and chips in Church. He had a small dining room once, where you could get fish, chips and peas and a slice of bread. If he liked you, you got best butter; if he didn't like you, you got margarine. I think it cost sixpence [2.5p].

Then there was Pete Chapman who worked at Blythes for a time then went to English Electric. He had a very intelligent dog called 'Blackout' and he used to go for a walk with my uncle Billy every Sunday morning. They ended up in Great Harwood after a day of 'dicing' [betting on dogs]. There was a lot of whippet racing in those days. They only had enough money for bus fare home so they said, 'We'll walk it and send the dog home.' They walked over the 'switchback' at Clayton-le Moors and they went along the bottom of Mercer Park and up through the

Dunkenhalgh. There was a heavy shower of rain so they were both wet through (Billy and Pete).

When Pete got home his dog wer lying on the doormat and it wer soaking wet as well.

Then there wer Billy Dowthwaite, the barber. It wasn't just a matter of having a haircut; it was like the local Community Centre! Everybody knew one another; that's why I don't believe in all these supermarkets today. The corner shop may have been coppers dearer but the shopkeeper would know if one of her customers had not been seen for a while and so could check that all was well.

From St. James Road to Maden Street, and along Henry Street there used to be forty-six shops. Miss Mooney the herbalist on Church Street was a character; she had a very gruff voice. 'Walt Endy' a farmer went in the shop; he said that one of his cows was constipated. 'I'll make a bottle up' she said, and she did. Apparently, however, Miss Mooney had given the farmer the wrong bottle and another constipated customer was on the toilet for two days! There were two men, used to save up to go on holiday and they'd be lucky to have ten bob [50p] spending money between them—but they still came back with a pound. Herbert Taylor came from up Stanhill, he was in the First World War. He liked to play dominoes and he usually worked nights at Copy Clough sewage works. Well this Saturday night, the men were having a drink, and they started to talk about ghosts—just before Herbert went to work.

'No such thing' he said. The argument went on and on; anyhow Herbert started off for work about 9.45 p.m.; me and Bill borrowed a white sheet off George Blezzard, the landlord, then we went into the churchyard and we heard Herbert coming down whistling 'Madamoiselle from Armentieres.' We jumped and shouted, 'Woo!'— talk about sprinters! he told us later he'd seen a ghost and we daren't tell him—he'd have killed us! When we were young, I'm ashamed to confess that we took jam jars off the graves in the churchyard which were used to put flowers in. We took the jars back to the shop where we were given a penny which we paid to go to the pictures. We would replace the jam jars on the grave when one wer empty. We had to make our own fun, there wer no radio er television.'

Do you remember any rag men?

'Oh yes—Freddie Mampy (his real name was Bancroft.) There was also a man, Fred Swift, who used to come round selling fish from a cart. His last calling shop was the Thorn Inn. The gates were on the chuch then and he allus gave us a 'belt'; why I don't know! Anyway, one day we wheeled his cart into the churchyard; took the horse out of the shafts, put the shafts through the gate then put the horse back. We watched him trying to get the cart out and we were all laughing.

One time when I came home on leave I went to Billy Downthwaites

for a hair cut. It was on a Sunday, and after church I asked him to cut mi hair—then we went in the Queens Hotel (that pub did a lot for charity then). Ronnie Whiteside had it and Pete Chapman was in; Alf Taylor, Ratcliffe Riley etc—all the 'Churchers'. They had a swear box in that pub and if you put a shilling in you could swear all dinner-time if you wanted and it all went to charity. I remember three of us going to the Rovers football match. We went into the George and Dragon after the match. Alf Crabtree wer with us and he always wanted to sing although he couldn't sing fer toffee. The pianist asked him what he wanted to sing and he sang 'Laura'. Well, he broke down umpteen times. Joe Carter said: 'Alf, the pianist can't play to you.' At that moment the landlord came in to tell us that the pianist played in the Hallé Orchestra! Coming back on the tram Joe got off at the Red Cap to go to the toilet and got left.

I used to go to mi aunt Kit's every Monday to mi tea. I'd be six or seven then and she took me to the Queens Hall picture place. Owd 'Thal Westwell' played the piano (silent pictures then). When there was a cowboy picture we'd clap and stamp our feet. Mi aunt Kit was a typical Irish woman; she would never eat meat on a Friday.

Then there was old Mr Wilson who lived on St. James Road; he was an old councillor. Mrs Wilson did a lot of work for the church and the people of the neighbour-hood. He was terrified of rats so he employed a rat catcher every Sunday morning. The rat catcher was called John Bill Riley and he came from Clayton-le-Moors. He came about 9 o'clock and he brought his rats with him. He then 'found' three rats and got paid fer them! There was a Mr Jackson who worked at Steiners; he brewed his own beer. He started work at 6 a.m. and took his beer in a 'kit'. There was Percy Lewis who

worked fer Church Council; one of the most conscientious road-sweepers I ever met. He took his brush home every night so no-one else could use it.

Mr Sleddon, who lived down Canal Street was a trawler man; his wife had only one leg. When he came home from his fishing trips everybody on Canal Street had fish. He used to 'borrow' and I've seen his old-fashioned kitchen where the wash boiler was. There would be broth in the boiler and a sheep's head. Another chap used to come to church; he contributed every week but he only went to church on Christmas Eve. He'd come to church with his bottles of 'Owd Ben' in a bag. He knelt down, said what he had to say and was away before the choir got to the bottom of the steps. When the choir sang 'Hark the Herald Angels Sing', he wept buckets. He came out of church, shook hands with the minister and said: 'It wer a bloody good service wer that, I'll see you next year.'

When you came back from the army, what sort of work did you do?

'I went to Foxhill Bank, printworks. When Foxhill closed, I went to Howard and Bulloughs, then English Electric; Blythes; Shopfitters, for about three weeks; then I finished up at Mastabar fer twenty-odd years.'

What do you remember about Hogans who had the paper shop?

'Well, Sally's still living; that woman did a lot of good charity work in Church unknown to anybody. There wer a lot of good people; Mrs Wild; Chrissie Rogan; Mrs Howarth; the Sisters at the Paddock House Convent. There was a good committee at the church for the old people. I was always interested in the Scout movement; we had no really bad lads, just one or two 'harum scarums'. It breaks mi heart today to see all the good work done in the past just go to waste. They've no leaders today, they all want paying for what they do.'

Tell me about the Church Urban District Council. When did you go on?

'I was elected in 1968 and I was Chairman in 1971/2. Later I was Hyndburn Housing Chairman, and what a mess it was in! My time is up now—certain things have improved since Church went in with Hyndburn Council; other ways have not. The old Urban District Councils had their own way of working; we were told that amalgamation would make things cheaper. I'll listen, then I'll give my side of the story. We used to have one health inspector for each district; today we have dozens!

They always say what's wrong with the country? Well, I've always been a fair-minded chap. First of all, family life has gone; morals also have gone, and that's where the decline started. I once saw some nursing sisters—we brought some of them home on the ship I was on and they were in a terrible state! I saw a child in Lubeck; a displaced person, a little girl. I often think about her; she had a beautiful face just like the Madonna. I was a sailor but I still can't swim. There was always that comradeship among us, though. Today everyone is for themselves, they are 'money mad'. I've never been on the dole; I've been on short time but I wouldn't sign on. I used to get on mi bike and go to the Lake District fer work. I knew a farmer who used to allow me to pitch mi tent and his wife would make mi dinner or give me a couple of rabbits

The 'Converzat' (a family dance and party) used to be an East Lancs event in Ernest Street; but they don't amuse themselves today,

they won't walk—they must have wheels! Television is the biggest evil of this age; I stopped in with this child last Tuesday, and the language! I switched it off; it was embarrassing. A lot of programmes want banning. I don't believe that state aided schools should be discontinued either. All this vandalism, in schools, I blame the parents; thi don't watch what their children are doing.

Owd Joe Kelly; he was chairman of Church Council twice. He had the shortest council meeting on record; about one and a half minutes! Then he went across to the Navigation Pub to play dominoes. Night after he had to go somewhere which meant wearing his chain of office.'

Did you know Bob Fielding?

'Yes, he worked in the canal yard; he must have loaded tons of Howard and Bulloughs machinery onto the boats.'

There used to be a tip at the Dunkenhalgh Walk, didn't there?

'Yes. That was the tip for Steiners and the paper mill. I've seen hundreds of folk come out of the church after the 6.30 a.m. service wearing shawls, and prams at the door; even some with clogs on going to the factory. There were many mills in Church once-over even one over the canal bridge called 'Davies's'. There was little Herbert Bullock who took bets. Police picked him up and he went to court. Walter Holden was on the bench he says—'very serious offence this' and he fined him two quid. When they came out of court Albert said, 'Here Walter, here's your bet for yesterday.' Uncle Charlie used to stand with his back to the fire and sing all the old songs.

Ramsdens who lived in Blackpool Street used to have a spiritualist come every Wednesday

night and a few of the neighbours went in. They had gas lights and one upstairs had no mantle on. The lads wanted to go out and offered a shilling to anyone who would 'get shut' of the spiritiualist. Me being small, I had to go under the table when the seance was in progress and I knocked under the table as the light flickered. The woman ran out saying, 'this house is haunted I'm not coming here again.'

I used to get to the Palladium with a bag of toffee (I didn't smoke then), and get change out of a sixpence. Church Council used to tip down 'Farhoons' and Howard and Bullough had the tip on the other side. Good Friday going down the Dunkenhalgh it was like going to a football match. We were all going to Whalley Nab. All our lives were built round the church and the school.'

Were there any cloggers' shops in Church?

'There was Mortons near the bridge up Market Street, Gascarth in Grimshaw Street. Then there was a clogger and shoe repairer in Henry Street. There were nine butchers' shops in Church, and six paper shops. There was a tripe shop on Bank Street, and there is a lot of land in Church which belonged to Church Council.

Rector Stephens bought the chain of office for Church Council. I never bothered to wear it. Owd Mrs Golden (God bless her), came to my inauguration.

She said: 'You were always a little devil at school. I don't agree with your politics, but Church Council could not have a better Chairman.'

I'd have given her my Chairmanship if she hadn't had a vote.

One day I was sitting round the fire with Mrs Holden and autie Bella. Owd Mrs Mayor was camping th'owd 'uns, and auntie Bella was crocheting like hell—she never dropped a stitch, talking and supping her stout. Auntie Bella had a rope burn on the side of her face, because when the horses used to pull the boat, she got caught with the rope which burned her.'

Do you remember the Dr. Harbinsons, father and son?'

'Yes. The son retired to North Wales and his daughter, Fiona, wore clogs. I once papered a house for one lady and when I moved the wardrobe there wer enough gin bottles to float a ship! I put them all along the skirting-board. 'That's my medicine' she said. One of her brothers fought in the Dardenelles and later he went to China; he used to come over sometimes. He used to have the lads racing to Church Kirk, the winner got one shilling, which was a lot of money then. He was interned by the Japanese and later married a Chinese woman but he dropped dead on his way home!

Walt Lomax was a farm labourer—but talk about a tailor; invisible mending; he could do anything, but he was a fool to himself.

Freddie Mampy was once up at court for stealing his donkey and all the lads went. Joe, the policeman said: 'be quiet.'

'Now' said the magistrate, 'you stole this donkey didn't you?'

'No I didn't I acquired it,' said Freddie.

Harry still has a marvellous sense of humour in spite of everything, and he's just as keen to work for the community and the people of Church even though he's no longer on the Council.

||||||||||||||||||||||||||||||||||||||||||||||||||||||||

Tales of Pat Again

from Joseph Holden, Oswaldtwistle

||||||||||||||||||||||||||||||||||||||||||||||||||||||||||||||||||||||||||||||||||||||||||||||||||||||||||||||||||||||||||

WHEN the brewery waggons were supplying the pubs in Fielding Lane they left the barrels not being delivered to those in the lane at the bottom near the Vicarage.

One day when Pat was working on the houses being built then at the bottom of the Lane, he pushed all the barrels into the vicarage yard and said to Betty O'Nibs as she passed: 'See there Betty, and there's one load gone away, it'll tek a few collections to pay fer it.'

I heard the tale that when he lived up on Cross Edge, his landlord wer Jim Holgate who had a joiner's shop o'er t' brig at Church. One day Pat went to him and asked him to put a thresher on his door. 'Nay, Pat,' said Jim, 'tha doesn't want me to walk reight up on yon wi' a bit of a thresher, does ti? Just tell me about what size of a piece o' wood tha wants and I'll cut thee a piece and tha can fix it thisell.'

Pat scratched his head and said: 'Well! I don't know anything about size, but there were two sheep on t' hearthrug when I geet up this morning.'

Early this century the pubs were open all day—some even before the factories started at six o'clock in the morning. One morning, Pat, who was having a day off, slipped into the Plough Hotel fer a pint, when he noticed that the landlord [Jem ut Plough] had got a dog—a setter.

'Fine dog you've got there, Jim,' says Pat.

'The damned thing won't look at watter,' said the landlord.

'Oh no,' said Pat, 'That breed o' dogs love the water.'

'Well,' said Jim, 'There's a couple of pints fer thee if tha gets it swimming.'

'Right, I'll take it up to Jacob's Lodge.'

And he takes out the dog to his home next door where after a pipe o' bacca and what he considered a reasonable time he threw a bucketful of water over the dog and led it back into the Plough.

'There you are Jim, I told you he wer a swimmer,' and soon polished the first pint off. But as the landlord was pulling the second pint, the dog walked around to his side of the bar.

'Why Pat,' he said, 'it's dry underneath,' indicating the dog.

'Sure it is,' said Pat, 'And isn't it a wonderful back swimmer!'

||||||||||||||||||||||||||||||||||||||||||||||||||||||||||||

An Ossie 'Gobbin'

||||||||||||||||||||||||||||||||||||||||||||||||||||||||||||||||||||||||||||||||||||||||||||||||||||||||||||||||||||||||

AN Ossie Gobbin wasn't a simpleton as people seem to think.

'Gobbin' comes from material found at Town Bent. When the Irish navvies were laying the main road through Oswaldtwistle they ran out of road material just at the lamp which stood where the library is. The Irishmen found this other suitable material at Town Bent and they called it 'Gobbin'. And now anyone who lives above the lamp comes from 'Gobbin Land' and they are affectionately known as 'Gobbiners'. The Oswaldtwistle clog-dancers (none unfortunately come from Gobbin Land), have a dance called the *Gobbiners Jig* and two other dances they perform are *The Ossie Jig* and *The Oswaldtwistle Hornpipe.*

Oswaldtwistle is split into four. Top End (Gobbin Land), Bottom End (Below Lamp), West End and Stanhill. Each section of people are proud of their own area but they are even more proud that they all come from Oswaldtwistle itself.

This information was given to me by an old man who has since died.

||||||||||||||||||||||||||||||||||||||||||||||||||||||||||||||||||||||||||||||||||||||||||||||||||||||||||||||||||||||||

An early tram on Blackburn Road, Church